Brassey's *Master Class*

Also from Brassey's:

Brassey's Book of Camouflage
Brassey's Book of Uniforms

Brassey's History of Uniforms

American Civil War: Confederate Army
American Civil War: Union Army
Napoleonic Wars: Wellington's Army
Napoleonic Wars: Napoleon's Army
Mexican-American War 1846–48
English Civil War
Roman Army: Wars of the Empire
Barbarian Warriors: Saxons, Vikings, Normans
Spanish-American War 1898
World War One: British Army
World War One: German Army

Brassey's Master Class

Master Modellers

Brassey's *Master Class*

Living History

By Philipp J. C. Elliot-Wright

Series editor Tim Newark

Brassey's London

For my wife Caz for putting up with my obsession with bringing history to life, and to Howard Giles who bears the responsibility for recruiting me into re-enactment back in 1971.

Copyright © 2000 Brassey's

First English Edition 2000

UK editorial offices: Brassey's, 9 Blenheim Court, Brewery Road, London N7 9NT
UK orders: Littlehampton Books, 10-14 Eldon Way, Lineside Estate, Littlehampton BN17 7HE

North American orders: Books International, PO Box 960, Herndon, VA 20172, USA

A member of the Chrysalis Group plc

Philipp J.C. Elliot-Wright has asserted his moral right to be identified as the author of this work.

Library of Congress Cataloging in Publication Data available

British Library Cataloguing in Publication Data
A catalogue record for this book is available from the British Library

ISBN 1 85753 283 X Hardcover

Typeset by Hedgehog, Upton-upon-Severn, Worcestershire.

Printed and bound in Spain.

Contents

Introduction

The recreation of historic battles for commemorative purposes has had a long history. There are accounts of the ancient Egyptians, Greeks and Romans re-creating, for mass public entertainments, various great military victories. In more recent history, King James II had the siege of Budapest re-enacted on Hounslow Heath in 1687 for the public in order to commemorate the participation of his natural son, the Duke of Berwick in this event. During the Napoleonic Wars, both regular and militia units often staged battle displays in Hyde Park and elsewhere for public entertainment and reassurance.

The modern version of this ancient tradition has its origins in the 1960s, when, in both America and Britain, a mixture of civilian and serving military personnel began groups dedicated to re-enacting particular periods of military history. In both countries this began with re-enacting their respective civil wars. In Britain, Brigadier Peter Young led the way with the founding of the *Sealed Knot* in 1968 and by the early 1970s various periods were being re-enacted, ranging from Ancient Romans to Medieval knights, the Napoleonic Wars, up to the American Civil War.

As with all new movements, the early stages were more about enthusiasm than authenticity. Commemoration rather than re-creation was the name of the game. Be it Viking, English Civil War, Napoleonic or American Civil War, nylon jackets, fibre-glass armour, velvet doublets and modern shotguns were standard. Displays tended to be lightly scripted melees similar to Sunday football rather than concerning itself with period drill and tactics. By the early 1980s though, re-enactment, as with much of the heritage industry, was maturing with authenticity and quality the guiding principles. Some groups, such as *The Ermine Street Guard* and *The White Company*, have come to be praised by professional archaeologists and historians for the quality of both their own research and appearance. Some of the research being put into reproducing given periods can even be found written up for academic publication. Activities have also became very varied, with not just battles but domestic living history and military encampments. Over the decades this has generated a whole army of highly skilled craftsmen and women to supply the necessary items.

Re-enactment has also played a key role in popularising our heritage, with many a green field or pile of crumbling stones costumed transformed into living history by enthusiasts. Today, some 400 groups exist, recreating almost every era of history and ranging from the 6,500 members of the *Sealed Knot* commemorating the English Civil War through to just a few dozen in living history groups such as *Histrionix* who focus on the domestic life of the eighteenth century. This tremendous growth in the hobby has witnessed its various manifestations becoming a key part in the promotion and display of historic houses, castles and museums. Many have come to realise the potential of re-enactment to bring an otherwise static historic site or museum display to life, thereby attracting the public. English Heritage has a *Special Events Unit* dedicated to organising a programme of living history and battle re-enactment events across the country at numerous sites.

To support both re-enactment groups and historic locations seeking reproductions of 'authentic' items, there has evolved an increasing number of skilled craftsmen and women who could manufacture the necessary historical items. Utilising historical research, most taught themselves how to manufacture an enormous range of objects and clothes from Roman armour, Viking weapons, Renaissance plate armour, Napoleonic shakos through to First and Second World War uniforms. Today, almost anything can be obtained, made to a quality that is often indistinguishable from original pieces.

This book is about some of the groups who utilise these objects, how such items are researched and made and the practical insights into contemporary usage that are consequently obtained. The objective is to provide an account of how re-enactment now provides a comprehensive account of military developments from Iron Age Britain through to the Second World War. In relating this I have focused on certain societies/regiments that offer a window on particular key periods. Consequently, *The Ermine Street Guard, Brigantia, Britannia, Regia Anglorum, Conquest, The White Company, The Fairfax Battalia, The 21eme Ligne, The 33rd and 68th Foot, The 55th Virginia and 18th Missouri, Pershing's Doughboys, The Great War Society* and *The World War Two Living History Association*, are the highlighted groups. It must be stressed that this choice is not to suggest any superior excellence over other societies or regiments of similar periods. Rather, they each offered the necessary detail for a particular historical transition. Inevitably, literally hundreds of groups are omitted in the text. Consequently, I have tried to mitigate any suggestion of favouritism by listing a range of re-enactment groups in the concluding directory. If I have omitted your particular group my apologies.

To understand how accurate reconstructions are arrived at it is necessary to appreciate the tremendous amount of academic research that is required. For the ancient and early medieval period, the archaeological record is fundamental, supplemented to a significant degree by sculptural sources. A mixture of the archaeological record, surviving artefacts, funeral effigies and analysis of contemporary archives underpins later medieval reconstructions. For the modern period, surviving artefacts and written evidence in the form of the exacting requirement of regulations is far more plentiful,

supplemented by photographs and film as one approaches the present day, leaving ever less room for errors in interpretation. However, the sheer volume of material requires a mixture of informed selection and educated conjecture as to what represents the 'average' soldier.

The various societies chosen to represent their specific period have each sought to familiarise themselves with the respective source material prior to any reconstruction. In this way they form a fundamental link between the academic and the practical, often providing vital empirical insight as to how evidence might be interpreted. Inevitably, given the varied nature of historical material for each period, the text reflects the differing approaches adopted for reconstructions by the respective groups. Rather than attempting to cover the entirety of each period, the first eight chapters primarily focus on how the 'average' soldier of each era has been reconstructed. The final chapter looks at those who might be termed 'specialists', who specifically reconstruct the demanding disciplines of artillery, cavalry, medicine and encampments.

One of the most remarkable Roman formations was the 'tortoise' (*testudo*). By locking their shields tightly together a near impenetrable shell could be rapidly formed. This allowed the legionaries to approach enemy fortifications protected from missiles and other heavy objects before they stormed the defences. Ermine Street Guard.

Romans and Celtic Warriors

Possibly the earliest period of British history to re-enact is that of the Iron Age Celts and the Roman invaders who were the first ever to successfully conquer this island. Each side of this equation offers elements of the essence of the soldier through history, the fierce individualistic warrior spirit of the Celts counter-poised against the stoical and disciplined ranks of the Romans. In their modern re-enactment guises, the various societies and groups portraying these stark contrasts closely identify with their respective forbears.

In 1972, one of today's most respected historical groups, the *Ermine Street Guard*, was formed. From its inception its objective was to bring to life, with as much accuracy as is humanly possible, every detail of the Roman soldier of the first century AD. With the initial assistance of Russell Robinson (author of the long definitive *The Armour of Imperial Rome*) who shared his extensive knowledge derived from his experimental reconstructions, the *Guard* committed itself to make by hand in the original materials exact copies of equipment from surviving pieces and other sources of evidence such as Trajan's column. Today, the membership of the *Guard* hovers around 45 and their total commitment to accuracy is recognised by professional archaeologists as a valuable form of experimental archaeology. The military profile of the society generally comprises two mounted cavalrymen, eight or nine auxiliaries and five or six officers, with the rest as ordinary legionaries. There is also a small domestic team composed of two or three women with a civilian male. This aspect is intentionally kept on a small scale in order not to distract from the *Guard's* primary goal: to recreate the Roman Army.

The *Guard* prides itself on being able to make every single item of arms, armour, clothes and footwear from within its own ranks to museum standard as, in addition to regular re-enactors, the *Guard* also have associate members, many of whom are drawn from the academic world. Support from this quarter is a two-way street, enabling the *Guard* to keep apace with the latest findings while feeding back practical insight gleaned from regular drilling with the equipment of the Roman Legions. For example, its detailed reconstruction of a catapult not only impresses the public at displays with its ability to shoot bolts into targets, but it also answers the question of actual range and accuracy.

The *Guard* incorporate a large variety of equipment within their ranks (new tools and artefacts for the military camp are being produced all the time) reflecting their belief that the Roman Army was, like all armies, in constant evolution. There is a tendency to perceive the ranks of any regular army as being equipped in a uniform manner, be it in the ancient or modern world. In practice, apart from elite palace guards, 'uniformity' in the Roman Army meant that all the soldiers had serviceable helmets, weapons, body armour and a shield that displayed the relevant unit emblem. The Romans certainly continued to use pieces of old equipment until they were worn out and beyond repair. Thus older styles remained in use long after newer ones began to make an appearance. Indeed, in a first century legion one would probably have been hard pushed to find any two men who were identical in terms of equipment.

In seeking to ensure authenticity in reconstructing the arms, armour and clothing of the first century AD Roman soldier, the *Guard* and other similar groups have a wealth of archaeological and contemporary artistic sources unparalleled by any other ancient period. For example, an enormous variety of swords, helmets and numerous other objects dating from the Flavian period have been dredged from the River Rhine at Mainz. These relate to the Legio XIIII that was in garrison at the fort at Mainz at that period, these items being lost when ferries capsized crossing the river prior to the construction of the bridge. Given the significant variation in design of these finds, it reinforces the belief that considerable variation in

The Roman legionary's two main weapons were the javelin (*pilum*) and sword (*gladius*). Having thrown their javelins, the legionaries drew their short swords and charged their enemy. The secret of Roman success was intense drill that gave them the ability to fight as a cohesive, close-order formation, even at the run. With the shield to protect almost the whole body, the short sword was used to thrust and slash at the enemy once contact was made. English Heritage.

equipment existed within units.

The familiar *caligae* (open leather sandal), for example, is generally recognised as standard issue to the legions and is certainly the style most commonly found at archaeological digs. By practical experimentation, the Guard has been able to estimate the average life span of a pair of *caligae* at around four months. However, it would not necessarily be accurate to equip everyone with *caligae*. Officers were entitled to wear *calcei* (a form of boot). In addition, it would appear that when serving in colder, damper climates the Romans tended to adapt general issue footwear according to local conditions. From finds at Vindolanda in the north of England it becomes clear that, certainly in Britain, legionaries often wore something more akin to a covered boot than an open sandal. This surprisingly comfortable leather, boot-

like footwear is now to be spotted among the ranks of the *Guard*.

Whilst from a distance the Guards' helmets and armour appear uniform, conforming to the stereotypical image of the Roman legionary, on closer inspection there are a multitude of subtle differences reflecting the evidence for variation. Very few complete helmets (*galea/cassis*) from the Roman Legions have survived as opposed to the multiplicity of fragments. Rather than fall into the trap of incorporating features from different examples, and thereby creating a fictitious hybrid, the *Guard* limit themselves to exact replicas of known examples. The most popular, and probably most common, legionary helmet type of the first century are those classified as 'Imperial Gallic' due to their obvious stylistic evolution from similar native Gallic examples. Their most distinguishing feature is the embossed skull reinforcements above the eyes in the form of stylised 'eyebrows'. The majority of surviving pieces are constructed from iron or thin brass, although three bronze examples also exist. Whilst bronze versions could have been more common in the Roman Army, because bronze was a costly metal in comparison to iron and softer than brass, obsolete or severely damaged bronze helmets were melted down for reuse. Thus the handful of bronze helmets discovered have been from rivers where they could not originally have been recovered. Iron helmets in comparison were just thrown away, being discarded along with other 'rubbish' after having their brass fittings stripped off. A significant factor favouring bronze helmets is that whilst bronze is less resistant to impacts than iron or brass, it is slightly lighter. However, it should be noted that the criticism by certain re-enactors of some reconstructions, that is, that helmets and fittings made from brass are substituted for bronze, is not supported by the archaeological evidence. Chris Haines of the *Guard* points out that overwhelmingly the finds point to brass being the commonly used metal during the first century, certainly for military equipment such as helmets, belt plates and hinges on armour, and for most decorations. In comparison, arguments for bronze are mostly supposition.

The short, double-edged *gladius* was designed for stabbing action although it could also be used just as effectively as a slashing weapon. The grip was carved from wood or bone whilst the large pommel could be either wood or ivory. The scabbards are made from wood bound in leather with brass fittings. A section of the legionary's buckled waist-belt (*cingulum*) can be seen beneath the *gladius*. Ermine Street Guard.

In addition to the Imperial Gallic line of helmets, mid to late first century legionaries would have worn those classified by the late Russell Robinson as of the 'Imperial Italic' type. These are similar to the Gallic types in general shape, but they lack the characteristic 'eyebrows' and have design features that indicate an Italian provenance, such as socketed 'twist-on' crest holders, side plumes and generally cruder workmanship. An early version of this is the 'Imperial Italic C', distinguished by its short horizontal neckguard, two different examples of which have been discovered in the River Po at Cremona.

Both Gallic and Italic styles of helmet from the first century have fittings to take a 'fore and aft' horsehair crest that were fitted just prior to battle. It is likely that this was a distinction of legionary rather than auxiliary helmets, although this is supposition due to the discovery of some helmets without fittings for crests. There is further conjecture that the crest colours might have varied from legion to legion or even from cohort to cohort. If so, along with

Whilst the *gladius* was worn on the right side of the *cingulum*, the dagger (*pugio*) was worn on the left. These weapons had a short, wide iron blade, whilst commonly the iron scabbards were highly decorated with enamel or silver inlay. Ermine Street Guard.

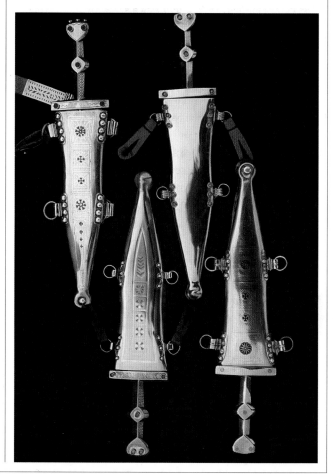

The centurial standard (*signum*) was a spear-shaft decorated with a number of silvered medallions. The centurial standard-bearer (*signifer*) was a soldier of exemplary character and good education. As he was the officer responsible for the legionaries savings he had to deal with detailed accounts. One of the distinguishing items he wore was a bearskin that was draped over his helmet and back. English Heritage.

At the head of each century was its commanding officer, the centurion, normally a man who had been elevated from the ranks. The distinction of the centurion was the transverse crest worn on his helmet, a shirt of mail or scale armour and a cloak of fine cloth. As can be seen, this centurion has received various decorations for bravery in the form of a pair of silver torcs and a set of silvered medals (*phalerae*) that were attached to the mail. Ermine Street Guard.

variations in tunic colours and designs on shields, it would have greatly assisted commanders in rapidly discerning the identity and location of specific Roman troops on the battlefield. However, they may have just been decorative rather than for identification purposes, as by the early second century the crest mounts were covered by iron cross reinforcements to the skull of the helmet. This may have been a response during the Dacian Wars where legions faced the greater impact of the scythe-like two-handed *falx*.

The body armour or 'cuirass' most readily identified with Roman legionaries is the flexible segmented or 'banded' armour, which was laminated, commonly referred to as *lorica segmentata*. For a long time there was much speculation and discussion as to how this armour was constructed until 1964 when there was a spectacular discovery at Corbridge in

northern England of a chest containing elements of at least six cuirasses. Whilst the Corbridge find is the only site where this type of segmented armour has been found in anything like a complete state, numerous other first century sites in Britain and across western Europe have revealed tell-tale evidence of cupric alloy buckles, hinges, hooks and loops indicating its widespread use. Although not as common in the East, given the generally warmer climate, archaeological evidence for segmented armour has even been found at first century sites in Israel, for example at Gamala in Gallilea.

That laminated-segmented armour is most commonly the type associated with Roman legionaries is due partially to carvings on ancient memorials such as Trajan's column, and partially to Hollywood. However, the early Roman legions wore mostly mail

This rear view of marching legionaries shows key details of both the flexible segmental iron armour (*lorica segmentata*) and iron or brass helmets (*galea*). The overlapping segments of thin iron sheet were linked internally by leather straps, and with hinged shoulder plates. They were arranged so as to deflect downward stabbing sword blows. The *lorica* weighed around 10 Kg. Equally, the helmet's deep neck guard was designed to deflect downward blows. Ermine Street Guard.

(*lorica hamata*), segmented armour enjoying only a relatively short life span of 200 years, before mail returned to dominance by the third century. Despite representing Roman soldiers of the first century, when segmented armour was at its height, practical experience and on-going research has caused the *Guard* to consider making more use of mail and scale armour (*lorca squamata*) among their ranks. Although the earliest examples of *lorica segmentata* have recently been found in Germany at the site where three legions in 9 AD were massacred under Varus, in fact the Roman Army never ceased using mail. Even during the first century, alongside some legionaries, the many auxiliary troops were only ever issued mail.

A factor in the initial popularity of segmented armour over mail was the comparative man-hours required to produce them. Contemporary Roman mail was manufactured with alternate-link punched and riveted rings, ranging in external diameter from as small as 3 mm up to 9 mm. Typically, first century finds have rings of around 5–7 mm external diameter. The time and expense involved is reflected by the many modern reconstructions that cheat by using 'butted ring' mail with rings considerably larger (in excess of 10 mm) than any ever discovered on an archaeological dig. Segmented armour represented a faster, cheaper option, taking 60–80 hours to produce a cuirass; about half the manufacture time required for a mail shirt. Unfortunately, segmented armour did require more maintenance, particularly during the rigours of campaign when the leather straps were prone to breakage through constant wear and tear. This has certainly been the practical experience of the *Guard*. Straps and small fittings such as hooks generally need replacement two or three times a year. However, in combat, segmented armour did afford significantly greater protection than mail.

Scale armour, whilst in use both before and after segmented armour, was generally inferior to mail and its popularity was apparently more to do with its attractive appearance than military utility. The sculptural record shows scale armour to have been very popular with officers, from the lowly centurion to the emperors. Contemporary writers referred to *lorica plumata* as an apparently more robust combination of scale and mail armour. A reproduction of this practical field version of scale armour was constructed using over 7,000 ribbed and tin-plated iron scales attached to a mail base of 5mm rings. It has proved the most protective and attractive of the entire range of contemporary field armours. However, it is also easily the heaviest and most expensive to manufacture and must certainly have been limited to officers.

As with armour, the types of sword carried by the *Guard* also vary, although this does not reflect any degree of historical controversy, either over type or construction. A very significant number of Roman shortswords (the *gladius*) have been excavated, and

there is a general consensus that by the middle of the first century the long-pointed version of Spanish origin had been superseded by the distinctly Roman type designated by historians the 'Pompeian' style. This has a parallel-edged blade and a short, clipped point. The blade is of diamond section, and can vary considerably in width and length. Consequently, around 75 per cent of the swords carried by the *Guard* are Pompeian style weapons, while the rest are comprised of a mix of Mainz and Fulham types (which have a longer point). Practical experience by the *Guard* has helped confirm why the Pompeian came to be preferred over the Mainz and Fulham swords, as the longer point on the Mainz and Fulham styles is more prone to breaking off. This inherent weakness undoubtedly contributed to the gradual dominance of the Pompeian sword within the Roman Army, as ever focused on practical matters, for the Romans favoured

In all lands conquered by the Romans, locally raised auxiliary troops (*auxilia*) quickly became a crucial part of the army. The attraction for recruits was the grant of Roman citizenship after 25 years of service that could be passed to their children and heirs in perpetuity. The auxiliaries here are light infantry (*cohors*) who were distinguished by a special uniform that reflected his unit's origin and specialist function. They wore simple mail shirts, with helmets, swords and daggers of a similar design to that of the legionaries although with less ornate decoration. As light infantry they carried a flat oval shield to ensure agility. Ermine Street Guard.

A lighter, more portable artillery piece was the *catapulta* that required only two legionaries to operate. Unlike the onager, this could be deployed on the battlefield where the small bolt it fired was quite capable of piercing amour. With a range of over 500 metres it could target specific individuals and was given the nickname the 'scorpion' (*scorpio*) due to the sharp 'sting' of the bolt upon impact as it tore into the body. Ermine Street Guard.

Roman military technology included a range of around seven sophisticated portable artillery pieces. Using the same basic principle of storing energy in twisted skeins of horse-hair and animal sinew, the various machines fired various projectiles, ranging from simple rocks to iron-tipped, armour-piercing bolts. Here two legionaries are in the act of drawing back the windlass and ratchet on a heavy catapult (*onager*) prior to placing a boulder in the sling that was attached to the arm. When fired there was sufficient energy in the skein to throw the projectile over the highest contemporary defences. Ermine Street Guard.

the style least likely to snap when plunged deep into the ribs of a struggling opponent.

The majority of swords excavated had a guard and pommel made of wood (long since rotted away on most examples) although a small number of blades with bone and ivory guard and pommel have survived. Regardless of the material from which the pommel and guard were constructed, all the grips appear to have been of polished bone and hexagonal in cross section. They were normally carved with ribbed segments to fit the fingers. If there is a criticism of some reconstructions it is that there is a tendency for the size of the pommel to be exaggerated.

Scabbards were made of wood and normally covered with leather. The sheet metal chapes at the throat and tip were usually decorated with pierced or embossed decoration. The scabbard was either suspended from an over-the-shoulder baldric, or attached to the 'military belt' (*cingulum*) girthed around the waist and worn on the right side. The evidence for the first century strongly indicates that swords were worn on the right side and predominately carried on baldrics. Again, the *Guard*'s practical experience has helped explain why. Experiments have shown that when carrying the shield in the extended left hand, if the sword is worn on the left side it constantly chafes against the curved surface of the shield (*scutum*), damaging both. This deduction is further born out by the historical evidence as by the third century, the curved-sided shield was superseded by the flat shield and the sword moved to the left side. Equally, the predominance of the baldric coincided with the use of the laminated plate cuirass and experiments have demonstrated that the military belt alone cannot satisfactorily support the sword when girthed over this armour. However, the military belt still played a vital role, as, by passing the baldric underneath the belt, it anchors the scabbard that would otherwise flap about. It also enables the sword to be drawn without the scabbard coming up with it.

A century of 80 men was composed of 10 'sections' (*contubernium*), each of eight men who shared a room at barracks or a tent on campaign. The eight-man tents were known as the 'butterfly' (*papilio*) and were made from goatskin. On the march, mules carried the tents and when the men halted for the night, the tents were laid out in the same strict order as at the fortress. Leaning up against one side of the tent is a legionary's marching pack that on the march was suspended over the shoulder on the wooden cross. The leather satchel contained such items as a razor, tools, eating utensils and personal effects. Ermine Street Guard.

Dangling at the front of the military belt was a group of metal studded straps with heart shaped terminals. The latter, whilst nominally to protect the groin area were as much for decorative effect.

On the left side, the military belt suspended the dagger (*pugio*), which, like the *gladius*, was of Spanish origin. The wearing of a dagger is another contentious area as some authorities on the first century suggest that it was no longer standard issue to legionaries. This is due to their absence from Trajan's Column and other monuments contemporary to it. However, the remains of military daggers have been excavated at later second century sites and appear on first century gravestones. Josephus also mentions them in his description of the Roman Army during the Jewish War of 66–70 AD. Ironically, those daggers that have been excavated have been highly decorated with enamel and metal inlay making such items one of the more complicated and time-consuming to reconstruct.

Alongside the familiar short stabbing sword of the Roman soldier, the other weapon most associated with legionaries is the throwing spear (*pilum*). As with swords, there is much archaeological evidence for their reconstruction. By the Flavian period the iron shank terminated in a hollow square-sided socket, as opposed to the flattened iron tang of earlier centuries. To give the *pilum* more force when thrown, weighted lead balls were added behind the square-socketed iron shank.

To complete the combat equipment of the average Roman legionary there was the characteristic curved-sided/tile-shaped rectangular shield (Scutum) with distinctive designs on its face. The *Guard*, along with most other Roman groups, bases their reconstruction on a fairly complete example excavated at Dura Europos in Syria, dating from the third century. This has a width of 83cm and a height of 102cm. However, other archaeological evidence indicates this was not a 'regulation' size as another, albeit less well preserved, shield from Dura is only 62cm wide by 93cm tall.

Fragments of a late first century Flavian leather shield cover and face from the camp at Vindonissa indicates an even smaller width of around 60cm. As with variations in the size of helmets and armour, the variations almost certainly reflect some degree of matching the height and build of the legionary to the shield they had to carry. The shield was constructed from three laminated wooden strips that were then encased in leather to add strength. The leather cover was made from two joined goatskins. At the centre of the shield was a square or rectangular metal shield boss (*umbo*) made from either iron or bronze.

That each legion had its own distinctive shield design there seems no doubt. Tacitus, in his description of the Second Battle of Cremona in 69 AD relates that two of Primus' legions successfully attacked a Vitellian catapult using the ruse of carrying the shields of the enemy legion. Although dating from three centuries later, the *Notitia Dignitatum* of 395 AD (an illustrated 'list of high officers' that detailed each

The *Ermine Street Guard* is not restricted to just male and/or military activities. The rich fabric of civilian life is reconstructed ranging from magistrates to doctors. Various female roles are reconstructed, particularly the many native British women who adopted Roman provincial dress and lifestyle. Ermine Street Guard.

generals command), depicted each unit's emblem in colour. Linked with the earlier evidence, this suggests a coherent and recognised system of legionary identification probably dating back to the late Republic. This may have also extended to the colour of the shield. The base colour of the Dura Europos shield was red and this may have been echoed in the tunic and crest colour. It is even possible that each cohort within a legion had a different colour shield with matching tunic and crest for identification purposes. The question for the *Guard* in recreating the shield design was how it was done. As expected from the numerous Roman sources, the Dura Europus excavated shield was encased in parchment-like goat-skin leather and subsequently, the contemporary pigments would not have adhered well to the smooth leather surface waxed or oiled to make it waterproof. Instead, the Dura Europos shield had a separate linen panel stitched to the front that provided an excellent material for the application of the complicated paint scheme. This is supported by further evidence from other excavated fragments of shield faces where the leather is perforated by stitch-holes. In addition, a separate hard hide leather cover was provided that was waxed or oiled to make it waterproof. This protected the shield from the elements on the march, although it was removed prior to battle.

In many respects the Roman Legions' secret weapon was mobility and much of a legionary's life could be spent marching from one end of the Empire to another. Consequently, one of the most lasting Roman legacies is their network of roads. As these legionaries are not carrying their packs and are equipped for combat they have not marched far. Legionary cavalrymen who could both scout ahead and act as messengers accompany them. English Heritage.

Whilst the *Guard* prides itself on utilising only extant examples of armour and arms for reconstructions, inevitably though there do have to be some compromises. Perhaps the most controversial question of debate within Roman re-enactment societies is the correct colour of the tunics worn by the legions. The *Guard* opt for red (white, blue, and other colours are in evidence with other societies) but accept that it is more a matter of preference. They have given up time-consuming experiments with natural dyes, as the colours so produced are, at best, an educated guess. The colour of shields and helmet crests are also, due to the same paucity of hard evidence, largely a matter of choice. The other principal compromise is the use of sheet steel for the armour as hand-beaten metal would be prohibitively expensive.

While the *Guard* performs in gleaming armour fit for any parade ground, they are the first to admit that armour on campaign would have been severely affected by local conditions. If a campaign was conducted in poor weather and the enemy was continuously harassing the legionaries, it would naturally have had a detrimental affect on the appearance of the legion. At the same time it must be borne in mind that the Romans made their armour and equipment to high standards. It was not only functional, but often decorative and beautiful too. There would be little point in producing work of this quality, honed to a high metal polish, if one merely intended to let it get dull and dirty in the field. There was also a psychological factor to consider, for when it came to real combat, as the Roman military commentator Vegetius said, 'The glitter of arms strikes very great fear in the enemy. Who can believe a soldier warlike, when his inattention has fouled his arms with mould and rust?'

Members of the *Guard* regularly spend over six hours cleaning arms and armour prior to taking it to a display. Back in the first century AD, the average legionary would probably spend about an hour working on his equipment after a day's march to ensure that it was kept free of rust and in proper trim. In peacetime even more effort would be devoted to

Most of what is known of the British Celts who faced the Romans comes from archaeology and the Romans themselves, given the Celts lacked their own written language. The reaction of the various Celt tribes to Claudius' invasion of 43 AD was varied. Some rapidly conceded to the greatly superior power of the Roman legions and concluded treaties with Rome. Other tribes resisted fiercely and at times succeeded in inflicting sharp defeats on the proud Romans who considered the Celts as little more than barbarians.
English Heritage.

maintaining the equipment. Officers ensured that the men kept out of trouble by limiting their *otium* (free time). Besides polishing their armour to a parade-ground shine, they trained with wicker shields and wooden swords (heavier than their combat equivalents). Attempting to reconstruct these wicker-training shields is another of the *Guard*'s ongoing projects. Having no surviving example to work from, they are proceeding by painful trial and error. Although early reproductions only withstood about a week's usage before they were more or less reduced to kindling, references have now been found to these training shields being covered in hide that has added considerably to their strength and durability. Despite making these wicker shields more robust, training

with them still results in various injuries, such as skinned knuckles and cut hands, as it must have for contemporary Roman legionaries.

The *Guard* also possesses the only example of an authentically constructed leather tent (*papilio*) as used by the Roman Army. Made of goat hides, this took 750 man-hours to construct (commercial costs for such labour intensive work would exceed £10,000). The Romans treated their leather tents with tallow, which was easily available and afforded good waterproofing. On campaign they were allocated one to every eight men (*contubernium*). Each *contubernium* was also allowed a baggage mule to carry the tent and other communal equipment (such as a corn grinder).

Working with other Roman re-enactment societies can also provide vital insights into the practical realities of legionary life. At a major event staged by English Heritage at Kirby Hall in 1997, the *Guard* collaborated with other Roman groups (*Legio Fourteen, Eight*, the *Antonine Guard*, the *Colchester Roman Society* and the *Gemini Project from Holland*). Formed as a single 'century' of 80 legionaries, the rattle of armour and accoutrements generated by the marching legionaries made it impossible for those at the rear of the column to hear the commands issued at the front. In order to dilute the confusion, an *optio* (the rank beneath a centurion) had to be employed to relay the commands. This has raised questions about whether Roman officers, rather than marching at the head of the column, might have positioned themselves (offset from the main body of men) midway along, from which position voice commands stood a better chance of being heard by all.

It is in this exhaustive detail that the high costs and dedication of Roman groups are most obvious. A single legionnaire's *segmentata* can cost up to £600 with the full soldier's uniform and equipment costing well over £3,000. This has two major consequences. Firstly, a member must become addicted to cleaning, as the arms and armour require constant attention. The second consequence is that Roman groups do not participate in physical combat. Even though there are some excellent Iron Age Celtic groups who would be happy to cross swords, such a contest is not possible. Firstly, even a single blow from a Celtic sword or spear

This selection of reconstructed Celtic artefacts demonstrates the range and quality of their craftsmanship. The magnificent torc, long sword and bronze helmet represent the range of Celtic skill in metalwork. Domestic artefacts are also present, ranging from a simple bucket through to horn items. The items themselves rest on wool cloth of typical Celtic weave.
Karl Gallagher.

could irreparably damage an item that can cost hundreds, if not a thousand pounds to replace. Further, the *Guard* carry weapons that have an authentic edge and as the Roman method of fighting involved first throwing the pilum and then charging in to thrust at the enemy with their *gladius*, it would offer too great a chance of serious injury to the Celtic re-enactors.

It would be unfair and inaccurate to suggest that the Celtic, or Iron Age groups as they prefer to be termed, are any less dedicated to accuracy and detail, but it is undeniable that they are motivated by a different spirit. One of the leading groups is *Brigantia*, which was formed in 1990. Representing the Celts from Southern Britain of the late La Tène period (100 BC to 50 AD) including those who confronted the Roman Claudian Invasion of 43 AD, they participate in numerous events each year, some alongside Roman groups. Mirroring their Roman counterparts, there is great attention to detail, with some of the warriors' elaborate torcs costing over £100 and swords over £200. Great care is taken to ensure the complex woad body patterns are as authentic to contemporary body painting as the limited historical record permits. Yet *Brigantia's* war cry 'Huru Ar Na Cheltigh' (victory to the Celts) reveals very much the essential attraction in the individualistic warrior tradition of the ancient

These two young Celts represent the ideal of these fierce warriors. The reconstructed sword being held by the sitting warrior is of the 'Anthropoid' type, its bronze hilt being based on one excavated at North Grimston, Yorkshire. Both wear the ornate torcs that epitomise the Celts' love of decoration and ornament. The most dramatic reflection of this Celtic trait is that both have reproduced the stunning designs that were painted and tattooed on face and body, their fearsome appearance being completed by their lime-washed hair. Karl Gallagher.

Celt. Effectively brought up from birth to be a warrior, the ancient Celt had a deserved reputation for ferocity and fighting at every opportunity, usually with each other. To this end, members of *Brigantia*, as part of their display, demonstrate Celtic fighting techniques and hence considerable training is engaged in outside of public events. As *Brigantia* engages in physical contact its swords and spears are necessarily blunted for safety, whereas those of Roman groups are very sharp indeed.

These respective differences between Roman and Celt produce comments from each side that leaves the observer feeling that the respective contemporary mentalities are being reproduced. Roman re-enactors, while respecting the care in attention to detail of the

Celts, tend to see them as having an over-aggressive, individualistic mentality and lacking group discipline. While the Celts see the Romans as over reserved and regimented, lacking individual sparkle.

As with research for the *Guard*, *Brigantia* relies on a combination of the archaeological, visual and contemporary (Greek and Roman) written records to provide evidence for their reconstructions. Similar to the Roman Army in one respect, the Celtic La Tène culture spanned Europe with particularly close links across the Channel between the British and their Belgae cousins. Thus finds and other evidence from across the Continent can be utilised in attempting to establish an accurate representation of how a Celtic warrior was clothed and equipped.

As clothing, wood and leather have, with few exceptions, perished in the intervening 2,000 years, it is rather ironic that it is the Greek and Roman sources that provide crucial information on aspects such as clothing and general appearance. The Celts of the La Tène culture lacked a written language, for although the Druids knew Greek and Latin, they were forbidden to write down any of their knowledge. Thus Greek and Roman sources, be it monumental friezes, pictorial or written material by scholars such as Herodotus, Lucan, Pliny and Julius Caesar provides vital evidence. However, care must be taken with these sources given both Greek and Romans considered the Celts to be 'barbarians' and a band of marauders. Nonetheless, once stripped of pejorative language, the broad commonality of their content indicates they are generally accurate. The contemporary Greek writer Diodoros Siculus described Celts as 'wearing striking clothing, tunics dyed and embroidered in many colours, and trousers that they call *bracae*: and they wear striped cloaks, fastened by a brooch, thick in winter and light in summer, worked in a variegated, closely set check pattern...Their wool is rough and thin at the ends and from it they weave thick cloaks which they call *laenae*.' This matches the image of a captive Briton on a fragment of a monumental bronze statue from Volubilis in Roman Mauretania in North Africa. The Briton's trousers are described as being of 'loud' and disparate check patterns whilst a cloak hangs loosely from his shoulders.

When Siculus provided a detailed description of

These beautifully reconstructed examples of Celtic torcs and pendants are typical of their type. Normally, two or more rods being twisted together and thickened at the ends made torcs. The Romans themselves placed great value on such items, ornate gold alloy torcs often being worn as trophies by Roman officers. Karl Gallagher.

Celtic arms and armour he naturally compared them to the contemporary Roman model he was familiar with: 'For arms they have man-sized shields decorated in a manner peculiar to them. Some of these have projecting figures in bronze, skilfully wrought not only for decoration but also for protection. They wear bronze helmets with large projecting figures that give the wearer the appearance of enormous size. In some cases horns are attached so as to form one piece, in others the foreparts of birds or quadrupeds worked in relief...Some of them have iron breastplates, wrought in chain, while others are satisfied with the arms Nature has given them and fight naked. Instead of the short sword they carry long swords held by a chain of iron or bronze and hanging along their right flank. Some of them have gold – or silver – plated belts round their tunics. They brandish spears that are called *lanciae* and which have iron heads a cubit in length and even more, and a little less than two palms in breadth: for their swords are not shorter than the spear of others, and the heads of their spears are longer then the swords of others. Some of these are forged straight, others are twisted and have a spiral form for their whole length, so that the blow may not only cut the flesh but also tear it in pieces and so that the withdrawal of the spears may lacerate the wound.'

Fortunately, Celtic funeral customs meant a

warrior's possessions were buried with him, thus numerous archaeological finds across Europe have provided artefacts, particularly the Celts magnificent torcs, characteristic long swords and war chariots, that fully corroborate Siculus' account. An excavated grave of a first century BC Celtic warrior at Owlesbury in Hampshire provided an iron sword, bronze rings from the sword belt, silver belt hook, large bronze shield boss, iron spearhead, iron ferrule and iron butt spike. The River Thames at Battersea preserved intact a magnificent second or third century BC bronze shield. This, along with a less complete version from the River Witham in Lincolnshire, demonstrates these shields were made from thin sheets of bronze on a wooden base.

The torc in particular highlights that the outstanding characteristic of the Celtic people was their love of decoration and ornament. The importance of their ornate torcs was fully recognised by Roman generals who listed them along with the military standards taken and took pride of place with the booty that was paraded through the streets of Rome. Being often made from gold alloy, beautiful examples of torcs have survived, for example, a whole group was found at Snettisham in Norfolk, with further sets at a dig in Ipswich.

It was not only the Celtic torcs that the Romans valued. It is often said that imitation is the sincerest form of flattery, and two aspects of Celtic arms demonstrate this. The distinctive Celtic bronze helmet, known as the Coolus 'jockey cap' due to its shape, so impressed the Romans that they adopted it. After the conquest of Gaul by the first century AD, it appears many of the Roman Army helmets were manufactured by Celtic armourers, and that it was from this basic Coolus type that later Roman adaptations evolved with crest attachments and cheek guards. Most fundamentally though it would appear that it was a Celtic armourer in Gaul who, in roughly the third century BC, invented linked metal rings to form ring mail. Rapidly adopted by the Roman Army, ring mail was to remain a fundamental part of any armour for almost 200 years, still being utilised well into the sixteenth century. Again, the emphasis of Celtic culture on craftsmanship and ornamentation undoubtedly played a crucial role in their being the progenitors of ring mail.

The archaeology also includes iconography, such as miniature figures of Celtic warriors and jugglers made by the Celts themselves (and therefore presumably accurate), and coins showing charioteers, naked and riding their chariot from the chariot pole, exactly as described in the Greek and Roman sources. There is also the iconography of the Greek and Roman triumphal monuments depicting victories over the Celts that reveal details such as trousers checked up one leg and striped down the other, shield designs and torcs.

Finally, the most striking aspect of *Brigantia's* appearance are the stunning designs painted onto the face and body of many of its warriors, alongside body tattoos and 'lime washed' hair. There is in fact limited evidence for the body paint beyond it being noted by Greek historians that the Celts painted their bodies with pictures of animals. There has been no corroborating evidence from archaeological finds, the well-preserved body of Lindow Man has revealed no evidence of woad or any other dye in his skin. Consequently, members of *Brigantia* turn to traditional Celtic art patterns for an appropriate source, using blue food dye applied by brush as the medium. The food dye has the advantage of soaking into the skin yet being easily washed out and if it rains, it does not stain cloth. The historic evidence for their smearing their hair with limewater is far greater, although experiments with lime have resulted in burnt scalps. Originally, Celtic warriors were able to neutralise the lime before it was applied by mixing it with urine. Not surprisingly, there are few takers in *Brigantia* for such a touch of authenticity so instead kaolin, a pure white chalk is purchased from chemists and when mixed to a paste with water produces the same visual effect without the need for any body fluids. To complete the effect, some members of *Brigantia* have had tattoos made, adapted from traditional Celtic designs found on metalwork.

The Dark Ages

When the Romano-British were finally told by Rome that they were officially on their own in 410 AD, the period in British history commonly referred to as 'The Dark Ages' began. Lasting from the conclusion of Roman administration until the arrival of the Normans in 1066, this span of history is now more accurately known as the early medieval period. These centuries witnessed the dramatic and crucial events that shaped the formation of modern England, Wales and Scotland. Firstly, the Celtic Romano-British kingdoms were defeated and displaced by the Anglo-Saxons between 409–793 AD. Driven to the West, the surviving Celts established what the Saxons termed the land of the 'Walsh', literally 'foreigners'. In their turn, the Vikings assaulted the English and Scottish kingdoms in the eighth century. This desperate struggle ended in final victory for the Saxons and resulted in a united English state by the ninth century. In the North, the arrival of the Gaelic-speaking Irish invaders from Dál Riada in Antrim (the original Scots) in the fifth and sixth centuries also witnessed the gradual emergence by the ninth century of a distinctive kingdom beyond Hadrian's Wall. By the eve of William the Conqueror's landing at Pevensey, the 600 years that had elapsed since Rome concluded its responsibility for Britain, had seen the establishment of today's distinctive English, Welsh and Scottish nations. Such major events have ensured this is a very popular period for British re-enactors.

Whilst groups re-enacting the later Saxon and Viking conflicts have been well established for many years, the earlier Romano-British period has, until recently, been neglected. The apparent lack of historical record and evidence making it appear an unrewarding period to recreate of. However a new society, *Britannia*, focusing on the centuries from the end of Roman rule to the foundation of the Saxon kingdoms, has swept away this negative perception. *Britannia* specialises in portraying Romano-British military and civil life from the fourth to the sixth centuries, a time during which the Western Roman Empire 'fell' and the ancient world gave way to the new medieval system, colloquially known as the 'Arthurian' era.

Unlike their counterparts recreating earlier and

In the decades preceding Rome's withdrawal from Britain, a series of forts were constructed along the south coast in response to the first Saxon raids. These light infantrymen, clothed and equipped as troops of the late Roman period, would have manned the forts on what became known as the Saxon Shore. The prominent crest on the helmet of the furthest soldier is based on an archaeological example. Matt Shadrake.

later periods, *Britannia* has been obliged to work without the benefit of a body of contemporary written works or an established body of tested archaeological evidence. Whilst the 'Arthurian' period has received a vast amount of attention from the mystical element in society, it has been largely discounted by most serious academics. As a consequence, the members of *Britannia* have had to embark on the equivalent of the 'needle in a haystack' search through sparse and scattered archaeological references, along with occasional documentary evidence from the handful of contemporary sources surviving from the decaying ruins of the Roman Empire on the Continent. It is a testament to their efforts that they have succeeded in constructing a convincing corpus of evidence for weapons, armour, clothing and equipment.

The sources have indeed been disparate. There is the late Roman military document, the *Notitia Dignitatum*, later Roman and Byzantine writers such as Vegetius and Procopius, and from contemporary

This fourth to fifth century Romano-British warrior wears a highly polished Sassanid ridge helmet that offered a considerable degree of protection from bladed weapons. The collar of armour protecting his shoulders from downward blows is lamellar and it is possible to make out the leather laces linking the iron plates. Dan Shadrake.

domestic Celts, a heroic sixth century battle poem, *Aneirin's Y Gododdin*. There is pictorial evidence, such as the wall paintings in the Via Latina in Rome, sculptural sources such as the Arch of the Tetrachs in Venice and numismatic references such as the recently discovered fourth/fifth century Hoxne hoard from Suffolk. By comparing the archaeological material to the artistic, it has been possible to sieve out the more fanciful and classical tendencies. For example, the ornate gilded crest and frontal eye pattern of a helmet depicted in the wall painting of a fourth century soldier at Via Maria Catacomb in Syracuse was not just artistic fancy, as an actual (non-gilded) version has been unearthed at Intercisa in Hungary. Without the Intercisa find, many would have dismissed the exaggerated crest as artistic licence inspired by classical convention.

Britannia has had to look abroad for many sources, both archaeological and artistic, for references for reconstructive purposes, and this has proved controversial. It begs an obvious question as to the universality of both clothes and equipment across the European Continent. The evidence suggests there were many similarities in both military and civil life for many decades after the collapse of Roman administration in the West, although the debate as to how long Britain retained its Roman identity is heated. What is not disputed is that the significant Roman manufacturing base and the network by which weapons and equipment were distributed collapsed. At the end of the third century AD, Diocletian had instituted imperial arms factories (*fabricae*) throughout the Empire manufacturing catapults, bows and arrows, longswords, spears, corselets, scale armour, shields and helmets. Whilst these provided a significant degree of universality to weapons and equipment, they did not survive the collapse of Roman administration. Rather, local British smiths, weavers, carpenters and the like continued to manufacture to meet demand using the recently departed late Roman items as their models. Consequently, whilst many pieces of late Roman equipment were repaired and embellished by local craftsmen, and lost, worn or broken items replaced, newer fashions were only gradually adopted. For example, in the famous Sutton Hoo burial in East Anglia, a richly decorated helmet of a Saxon king is obviously derived from a late Roman 'Ridge' helmet, itself a derivative of the Sassanid ridge helmet.

A major area of controversy for *Britannia* is the question of armour, both in terms of historical references and its reconstruction. Whilst the earlier centuries of the Roman Empire have a plethora of artistic and archaeological evidence, by the fifth

Offering an example of cultural collision, here the Sassanid ridge helmet is being held opposite the fine hilt of a fifth century Germanic style sword. The Romano-British warrior is wearing a coat of Lamellar armour over which the sword is carried on a leather baldric. Again, the leather laces linking each iron plate of the lamellar armour both horizontally and vertically are very obvious. Dan Shadrake.

century such material is almost non-existent. The breakdown of Roman administration and the commercial base that relied upon it broke down over a number of decades thus ending the mass production of armour. This left only a relative handful of native craftsmen with the knowledge and skill to manufacture and repair the lamellar and ring-mail armour of the late Roman Army. Whilst the situation did not change overnight, the local British militias no longer had a regular supply of armour and that manufactured locally was not of a consistent quality when continental sources of raw materials dried up and native and cheaper alternatives were adopted. Thus, whilst local kings and warlords inherited or could afford their own archaic armours, it is argued that leather became a common alternative for the rank and file. Favouring the argument that the mass fabrication of ring-mail links and scale armour ended, *Britannia*

has experimented with leather and horn in the tradition of experimental archaeology to demonstrate the practicalities of these materials. If correct, because such materials do not survive exposure to the British climate, it would provide a convincing explanation for the lack of archaeological finds.

Britannia, alongside several other research/re-enactment groups, have experimented with leather hide armour with the unexpected result that having been boiled, moulded to the shape required and then left to dry, thick hide becomes as hard as mild steel. This leather hardening process is often called *cuir-boulli*. In this altered form, leather is able to resist blows as effectively as most metal armours as well as being almost impervious to sharp blade thrusts. In fact, experience suggests that such leather armour is often able to absorb and disperse impact energy more efficiently due to its composition.

Given that the British climate has left no examples of such leather hide armour, *Britannia* has looked elsewhere, in this case to the two thigh defences of rawhide lamellar that were discovered at Dura Europos in Syria. These give weight to the ability of provincial military establishments to adopt leather hide as a practical alternative to bronze or iron, particularly as leather would be one commodity easily

This fifth century, heavily armoured Romano-British warrior wears a helmet based on one found at Burgh Castle. Unlike the previous ridge helmets, the hinged cheek pieces have been lined in leather for additional comfort. Reflecting the arms and armour of most Romano-Britons, he wears a mail shirt and is armed with a spear with an iron head. It is possible to make out the simple table weave pattern on the collar of the tunic he is wearing beneath his mail. The woman to his left wears a tunic, the cloth of which is woven in the common 'tartan' style. Derek Clow.

available in rural Britain. Utilising the Dura Europos evidence as a foundation, *Britannia* has manufactured a limited number of items. However, *Britannia* has not gone overboard on such pieces, as although leather hide armour is durable, lightweight and generally corrosion free, it loses most of its protective value if waterlogged. Given the general dampness of the British climate, be it rain, sleet, snow or mist, and numerous rivers to ford, it seems unlikely to have been widely used. It is also by its very nature quite inflexible and only practical for torso and upper arm and leg defences.

As opposed to the debate about the use and design of leather armour, there is no doubt about mail. The earliest archaeological examples date from fourth

century BC Celtic sites whilst a derivative form was seeing service in First World War and butchers and the like still utilise steel mail mittens. As mail is best at deflecting edged weapons rather than crushing blows, padded garments have usually been worn beneath the mail and both protective and decorative leather straps (*pteruges*) hung from it. Used mostly as body armour, by the fourth century AD, full-length coats of mail were common. However, its flexibility and durability ensured it was also utilised elsewhere. The 'Battle of Ebenzer' fresco at the Synagogue at Dura from the third century appears to show soldiers wearing mail coifs (a mail hood), as do the pictures in the *Vergilius* Vatican manuscript from the fourth century. Certainly, the sixth century Coppergate helmet has a mail Aventail (a curtain of mail attached by means of staples around the base of a helmet). However, some caution is required as the depiction of scale and mail by contemporary artists is rather confusing. Ancient artists, sculptors and jewellers tended to use a wide variety of techniques for these textures, including zig-zags, herringbone, dots or simply crude lines.

There seems little doubt that mail was worn throughout the fourth to sixth centuries, although with the collapse of the large scale Roman military manufacturing system it was just the Romano-British military elite who could afford to. The sixth century poem *Y Gododdin* by Aneirin describes an elite body of cavalry, '*Spear-shafts held aloft with sharp points, And shining mail-shirts and swords*'. The ancient method of manufacturing mail was both complex and time consuming. First, soft iron wire had to be drawn to a standard thickness, then wound around a narrow iron mandrel and this coil was then chopped off the mandrel using a cold chisel resulting in tiny open links of metal. Next, these links were forced through a narrowing hole using a punch causing the link ends to overlap and form a ring. These ends were then hammered flat and pierced so that a small wedge of metal could be inserted that would act as a rivet, sealing the link closed. With the raised rivet heads facing out, the mail was assembled with a standard four links through every one, the familiar pattern of mail soon appearing after the joining of just a few links. Even with modern tools and materials, for re-enactors of all periods, the construction of mail is just

This is a close-up of the table weaving used to 'finish' the tunic that was a common pattern in the Dark Ages. It also provides a view of the edge of the mail shirt that left the warriors neck and upper shoulder completely exposed to blows. It was this vulnerability that caused many to wear some form of armoured collar. Gary Sweeny.

as time consuming and laborious as it was for their forefathers. A single mail shirt could contain anywhere between 20,000 to 60,000 rings depending upon length and the diameter of the rings. Consequently, whilst some committed purists still insist on utilising just round section wire for their links, many choose dark metallic 6-8mm square section spring-washers that appear reasonably authentic. Whilst this choice is dictated by the practical considerations of time and money, and the need to be able to carry out rapid repairs, it is not without some evidential foundation. A fragment of stamped square section mail used alternately with round section wire was discovered at Carlingwalk Loch.

The way mail is manufactured, its significant weight, problems of repair and the inevitability of rust have encouraged many re-enactors, including those of *Britannia*, to research alternative types of metal body armour, notably scale armour. Compared to mail, scale armour is lighter and simpler to manufacture, although not as flexible or as protective. Hundreds of diverse examples of scale armour have been discovered from the Roman period, mostly made of bronze, with a tiny handful that are tinned or gilded such as that discovered in Chester. The size and shape of the scales vary, though from the few scraps of material found attached to them, fabric was the normal support. It

Mounting the staunch defence of Britain against the various enemies and invaders is this fifth century *limitanei* (frontier static troops). Men like him had manned the defences of third and fourth century Roman Britain, and after Rome withdrew, he and his compatriots remained to defend Hadrian's Wall and the Saxon Shore Forts. Equipped as a light infantryman, he wears a fur 'Pill-Box' hat whilst his waist-belt boasts a fine chip-carved brass buckle derived from German styles, again demonstrating the variety of influences on clothes, arms and armour at the time. M. Turner and I. Burrige.

This group of light armoured Romano-British warriors display the mix of styles that were common. Both warrior's kneeling at the foot of the wall have the popular Sassanid ridge helmets, whilst the soldier standing guard wears simpler style of ridge helmet. The standing figure carries a Germanic style sword on a baldric, the fine metal fittings of which are clearly visible. Their tunics display the various patterns derived partly (in the case of the standing figure) from Roman style or (for the figure on the left) Saxon and Celtic. Dan Shadrake.

was this, though, that mitigated against scale armour, as it was vulnerable to upward thrusts with swords and spears that can easily be driven underneath the scales to penetrate the fabric backing.

One of the best finds of scale armour was dug in 1979 from a pit at the legionary base at Carpow in Perthshire. A number of small bronze scales approximately 1cm across were excavated, a few still attached to their linen backing and with the scales attached to each other horizontally by means of wire links that were loosely passed through holes in the side of each scale. Each complete row of scales was then positioned on the fabric backing, a strand of yarn was passed over each set of upper holes and the thread that attached the scales to the fabric backing was passed

through one of the upper holes over the yarn and back through the remaining upper hole. This process was repeated on the next row, the armourer being careful to overlap the yarn attaching the row below.

As to appearance, the sixth century poet Aneirin referred to 'dark blue armour' in *Y Gododdin*. This is not felt to suggest the armour was painted but rather that it was so brightly polished it reflected the sky. Equally, the fourth century writer Ammianus referred to 'gleaming' armour. This could suggest the practice of gilding and silvering that was used throughout the Roman era onwards. This involved beating out gold or silver into a thin foil sheet and covering an object such as armour scale using a solder. Tinning was a much simpler process in which the armour components were dipped in molten tin, which as it has a lower melting

The *carroballista* (cart or wall mounted bolt throwing device) these warriors are preparing was one of the many items of sophisticated Roman military equipment that the Romano-British continued to deploy long after the end of official Roman rule. The warrior at the rear of the *carroballista* is wearing an example of scale armour. Visible at the back of both his Sassanid ridge helmet and that of the soldier kneeling at the *carroballista*'s base are mail neck guards, an early form of the *aventail*. Derek Clow.

When fighting in the field, Romano-British light infantry, like their Saxon opponents, used their shields to form a protective wall. Here the slightly better equipped warriors with polished Sassanid ridge helmets and swords take position in front of their lighter armed compatriots who mostly just have spears. Ideally, the warriors behind would thrust their spears over the shoulder of the front rank into the faces of their enemy. English Heritage.

point than bronze, would coat the object in tin producing an impressive silver-like coating.

The final type of armour of the period was lamellar, a distinct variation of scale armour that originated in the East. Roman culture was always adopting and improving upon ideas and innovations borrowed from other cultures, and the Roman Army was no exception. In fact, some historians have suggested that the longevity of Roman military success was partly due to this characteristic of willing absorption. Certainly, the enormous breadth of the Roman Empire ensured the cross-cultural exchange of far flung peoples including the introduction of to diverse military technology such as swords and armour, for example, the long slashing cavalry sword of the late Roman Empire, the *spatha* and the Sassanid

ridge helmet. The appearance in Western Europe and Britain by the latter part of the third century AD of Eastern lamellar armour is a perfect example of cross-cultural fertilisation in armour.

Lamellar armour consists of long narrow scales laced both horizontally and vertically to its neighbour. The advantage of this self-contained lacing construction is that it requires no leather or fabric backing. The modern reconstructions using hide, bronze or mild steel scales have proved relatively easy to produce even by the unskilled, with repair and maintenance equally straightforward. Practical experiments have proved that lamellar armour provides both a protective surface–blows against a single scale are absorbed by its eight surrounding neighbours–whilst still being remarkably flexible. A number of examples have been discovered in Britain,

two small round ended pieces being found at Corbridge. For *Britannia*, perhaps the most valuable and interesting find is the relatively large mass of iron lamellar plates, albeit rusted into a dilapidated cluster, excavated in Somerset. Here the average size of the scales is around 2.8cm wide by 5cm high. Of greatest value though is that due to the action of the sulphides produced by the corrosion of the surrounding scales, the structure of the actual leather lacing has been preserved as a positive cast. The leaching of the sulphides into the organic material, in this case leather, gradually replaced the original fibres whilst retaining their form. Although in poor condition, it provides an excellent insight into the construction of lamellar armour and conclusive proof that it was actually used in Britain. Thus, whilst the surviving evidence demonstrates there are a variety of lamellar plates and various methods of lacing, the Romano-British finds indicate that the most basic method of construction is appropriate for the majority of *Britannia*'s reconstructions. Consequently, in the absence of contemporaneous references, designs for complete suits of lamellar armour have been taken from slightly later depictions of Byzantine icons and numismatic evidence. Hence one particular reconstructed lamellar suit utilised a sixth century Lombardic or Byzantine silver plate, the 'Isola Rizza Dish', whose relief design shows a lamellar clad cavalryman in remarkable clarity. This uniquely revealed a shoulder-guard with a downward facing radial pattern of lamellar plates that were reconstructed without significant difficulty. However, with an eye to safety as the suit is for re-enactment purposes, the shoulder-guard was constructed with large belts and buckles for rapid release in case access was required for medical attention.

As with armour, there were various contemporary styles of military belts and fittings, some derived from late Roman military equipment, others from subsequent German influence. Thus members of *Britannia* wear a wide range of belts, ranging from the broader Germanic styles with copper alloy mounts and stiffeners, the earlier third century ring buckles and several plainer 'D'-shaped Eastern Roman examples. Most of what is known comes from graves and German burials offer the best insight into construction as their belts were commonly placed separately at the feet of the corpse, such as the fairly well-preserved Dorchester belt. This provides a better idea of the relative positioning of the buckles, studs, general fittings and sometimes even the dimensions of the leather itself. A fairly common buckle design of the period is the square fretwork bronze plate with a hinged buckle, often composed of two converging serpent or dolphin heads. The Colchester example is perhaps the finest piece in this category and has been reconstructed for use in *Britannia*. When mounted on a plain leather belt with contemporary (Richborough) 'propeller' stiffeners, this provides a convincing demonstration of how by taking components from

This fifth century group of both heavily and light armoured warriors defending the Saxon Shore might be termed as off-duty. In the background, leaning against the bushes, is a simple Christian standard that set the Romano-British apart from their pagan Saxon and Pictish enemies. Dan Shadrake.

different sources but a common cultural context, a convincing piece of reconstructed 'dark age' equipment can be reproduced. It is the modern reconstruction of these items in particular where the new generation of highly skilled, competent armourers are demonstrating that re-enactment has evolved as they reproduce the intriguing and flamboyant finds from the fourth to sixth centuries.

In many ways the final and most evocative piece of reconstructed equipment for *Britannia*, or any other ancient or medieval group, is the sword. During the centuries of the Roman Empire, because swords were regular army issue it detracted from their role as indicators of social status. However, with the progressive breakdown of Roman administration and organisation, swords again became expensive and hard to obtain. Consequently, they became almost exclusively the weapon of the warrior élite, be they Romano-British or Saxon. As a general rule, the members of *Britannia* recreating the Romano-British choose to all carry swords for two reasons. Firstly, so that they can demonstrate they are adopting a quasi-Roman style of equipping an élite fighting force, particularly the front rank. Secondly, as swords provide spectacle and excitement at public events thus allowing the recreated conflict to be prolonged for the entertainment and (hopefully) education of the

This Pictish woman wears an example of the simple shawl made from woven woollen cloth that many men and women of all cultures used to keep warm in Britain's chilly fourth to sixth century climate. It is held in place at the neck by a metal broach made in a traditional Pictish style. Lynne Smith.

audience. Although spears have their place, it is bladed weapons, but particularly the sword, that provide both varied and interesting fight sequences, be they random or choreographed, as compared to spears and shafted weapons in general.

As with helmets and armour, there have been numerous finds of late Roman and post Roman swords in Europe. This is fortunate for re-enactors in Britain as there have been only a handful of fifth and sixth century swords excavated in Britain and not one can be conclusively identified as Romano-British. This major problem of identification as to the cultural identity of finds is due to the fact that the majority of Romano-British were Christian or subject to very significant Christian influence. Thus, with Christianity's simpler burial rituals and its disapproval of pagan practices, personal belongings, including arms and armour, were no longer buried with the dead. Rather, they were handed on to other family members and warriors, thus being subject to regular

cycles of repair and alteration. Those few swords of the fifth and sixth centuries that have been discovered are generally identified as pagan German. Due to the steady influx of Saxon *foederati* (mercenaries) in the period before and after the Roman withdrawal, Romano-British military culture was saturated with Germanic influence and imports of not just swords, but belt buckles and numerous other Germanic accessories. This influence became even more pronounced with the arrival of Saxon, Jute and Angle invaders. Consequently, any sword or accessory identified as fifth or sixth century could equally have been the product of the Romano-British, Saxon *foederati* or German invader. Whilst it would thus be quite acceptable for *Britannia* to mix and match the cultural origins of its weapons and equipment, to enhance identity it chooses to standardise its Romano-British ranks so as to provide an identifiable contrast with its variegated opponents.

The broad range of sources and influence operating in the fifth and sixth centuries also means there was no one method of manufacture. Some were inherited from earlier periods, some from *foederati*, some imported from surviving centres of *fabricae* and some manufactured by local native craftsmen. Further, there was a distinct Pictish and Irish body of work given their geographical isolation from major influence by the Roman world. The 'Celtic fringe' of the Scottish highlands and Ireland retained something of the ancient La Tène culture, from which origin their swords had evolved. Thus swords with gently curved hilts and sturdy lozenge sectioned blades, dated to the third and fourth century, have been discovered at Edenberry, Co. Offaly in Ireland. However, this does not mean the Celtic fringe was immune to influence from several centuries of Roman neighbours. Various small Roman style *gladius* and *spatha* blades have also been discovered in Ireland, and such derived types continued to be manufactured there until the seventh and eighth century arrival of the Vikings and their influence. Consequently the Romano-British with their derived late Roman styles would have had contact with Irish and Pictish raiders armed with a mixture of evolved La Tène swords and bastardised

Some of the most ferocious opponents of the Romano-British (as they had been for the Romans) were the Picts who staged regular raids. Although this tattooed Pictish warrior is obviously less well equipped in comparison to his Romano-British opponents, lacking helmet, armour or even shoes, he and his compatriots more than made up for this by their ferocity. His simple round shield bears a traditional Pictish design. Dave Miles.

gladius and *spatha* from the north and west, and Germanic raiders and their weapons from the east.

The most justifiable source for early Romano-British swords is the late Roman period *spatha*. Not only are these found to occur throughout northern Europe, this type of sword reflects the move away from static infantry based battles towards the evolving emphasis on cavalry and thus the embryonic style of mediaeval warfare. As described by the late Roman military writer Vegetius, it was a Romanised evolution of the much earlier Celtic cavalry sword. The second century AD writer, Arrian in *Ars Tactica*, provides an account that both illustrate the *spatha* itself and its use in cavalry warfare. 'Of the Roman cavalry some carry pikes and charge in the manner of the Alans and Samatians and others have lances. They wear a large

By the seventh and eighth centuries the Saxons had comprehensively defeated the Romano-British. Whilst there was little to distinguish them in terms of weapons or armour from their Romano-British opponents, they had evolved their own distinctive styles. These Saxon warriors all wear the distinctive Coppergate style helmets which were of *spangenhelm* construction with cheek-pieces and nasal guard. In addition, the mailed warrior has a mail neck guard attached to the rear of his helmet as an early form of aventail. Dan Shadrake.

flat sword suspended from the shoulders and they carry broad oval shields, an iron helmet, an interlocked corslet and small greaves. They carry lances both to hurl from afar, whenever that is necessary, and to fight off the enemy at close range, and if they have to engage in close combat they fight with their swords.'

A distinctly late period Roman-style *spatha* is chosen for reconstruction by *Britannia*'s re-enactors, utilising the intact example discovered at the fourth century burial site at Cologne. This has a parallel blade of 28in long by 2in wide and a ribbed ivory grip. Convincing reconstructions have been manufactured utilising further archaeological finds of detached fittings, such as a hilt from Butzbach in Germany, in conjunction with the numerous sculptural representations. The late Roman sculptural

Having finally defeated the Romano-British kingdoms by the seventh century, the Saxon kingdoms were themselves subject to assault by the Vikings from the late eighth century onwards. Commencing in 793 with a raid on the monastery of Lindisfarne, Viking attacks soon transformed into a bitter war of territorial conquest. In terms of arms and equipment there was little to distinguish Saxon from Viking with most combatants armed with just a spear and a shield for protection. English Heritage.

representations are distinctly varied, for example, some have very plain hilts mirrored in actual contemporaneous archaeological finds. *Britannia* feels it vital that such parallel corroboration is available before it is utilised as a model for reconstruction.

In respect of contemporary blade technology, what is known of Roman construction indicates that at best, the quality of materials and manufacturer varied enormously from region to region. J. Lang in *Study of the metallurgy of some Roman swords* (1988) contrasts examples of higher quality composite blades, where softer iron of low carbon content is sandwiched between strips of carbonised iron (pre-industrial era steel) and poorer quality weaker blades of low carbon iron that do not employ the composite method. Thus when it comes to reconstruction modern armourers have the considerable advantage of consistent quality steel to work on as opposed to the irregular hand-worked iron of the pre-industrial smithies. In fact, given the punishment re-enactments inflict upon swords where blunt edged blades are struck against each other hundreds of times a weekend, using the materials and techniques of ancient armourers would be foolish, not to say dangerous. Furthermore, the original time consuming processes, such as pattern welding, would make swords prohibitively expensive (rather like the originals).

The main battlefield formation of both Vikings and Saxons was the 'shield wall'. With shields held rim to rim, or even overlapping, both sides would advance to contact with the spearmen and warriors with axes behind ready to thrust and strike over the shoulders of the shield-bearers. As contact was made the shields opened slightly to allow the front rank to thrust and parry with their swords. If both sides were resolute, gaps soon resulted as individuals traded axe and sword blows and a swirling melee quickly resulted. English Heritage.

As previously mentioned, for various reasons *Britannia* took a conscious decision to arm all its Romano-British warriors with swords. However, the far cheaper and simpler to make spear was the most common weapon of the ancient and early medieval world. As with swords, there were various contemporary designs, reflecting different functions; some for throwing, some for defence and some merely for training and hunting. Weight, size and style of head determine these differing functions. In referring to the later regular Roman Army, Vegetius describes a variety of shafted weapons, the *lanciae* (spear), the *spiculum* (throwing spear) and *plumbatae* (throwing dart). This variation is supported by the archaeological finds, of which there have been many, from late Roman and Germanic sites; a surprisingly high number being in the British Isles. Fairly plain, leaf-bladed examples from sites such as Catterick and Caerleon provide the basis for a general infantry and cavalry spear. These have fairly long sockets and rounded tips that make for safe and convincing re-enactment spears.

As with all periods of battle re-enactment, safety always comes before accuracy or spectacle. Thus all historic periods utilising bladed weapons have minimum thickness and point radius regulations to prevent penetration. Consequently, both in construction and use, swords and spears are not exact facsimiles of originals, but subtly 'safe' copies with blunted blades and rounded points. As a rank and file weapon, modern re-enactment has demonstrated how effective a weapon spears were, even in untrained hands. Provided they do not break, a close order wall of spears can hold off even heavily-armoured veterans. However, practical experience on the re-enactment battlefield has also revealed the spear's contemporary drawbacks. In a confined melee composed of two opposing sides locked in conflict the spear, if it cannot go forward, may be pulled back for another thrust or be pushed back by the weight of the opposing line. In both cases this can result in injury to the ranks behind. Throwing spears present an even greater problem if

This group of ninth century combatants are well equipped with many wearing mail shirts and early riveted *spangenhelm* helmets. Those wearing mail would have worn some kind of padded tunic under it to spread the impact of any blow. These garments ultimately became the gambeson. Although few Vikings or Saxons could afford a broad-bladed axe, those warriors that could possessed a fearsome weapon that could easily split open an opponent's helmet with a single blow. English Heritage.

they are to be both convincing yet safe. For example, a distinct spearhead discovered at Carvoran in northern Britain has a broad and barbed iron head at the end of a long shank thus echoing both earlier Roman *pilum* and contemporary German *angon* (both throwing spears). It is likely that it was originally used as both a projectile and hand held thrusting weapon. However, its heavy head with its sharp point and barbs makes its reproduction just too dangerous to use in battle re-enactment. As with all throwing spears, reconstructions using alternative materials with padded heads does not either look realistic nor strike the ground with anything resembling dramatic effect. Consequently such weapons are limited to living history displays where unmodified facsimiles can be safely used to demonstrate to the public their accuracy

and effectiveness.

Such concerns extend to the wooden shafts of spears that average between 6 and 7 feet. These were originally made of indigenous hardwoods such as lime, hornbeam (ironwood), ash or holly (the latter wood being specifically referred to in *Y Gododdin*). As these hardwoods are expensive, reconstructions often utilise cheaper woods. However, care must be taken that alternatives are not liable to shatter and split thus creating potential battlefield hazards.

Excepting the mountains of Wales and northern Scotland, by the late seventh century the Saxons had subjugated much of Britain and new 'English' kingdoms took root. Before the so-called Dark Ages drew to a close, the era's most feared warriors made their appearance in the guise of the Vikings. Although there were earlier raids, the first recorded attacks came in 793 and 795 with the assaults on the monasteries of Lindisfarne and Iona respectively. For the next 300 years, Viking raids on both Britain and Ireland became attempts at conquest and to this day they have left their mark on the north-east and East Anglia in the form of numerous Norse place names. It is often forgotten that the last Viking assault came after the Norman Conquest in 1085. Ever since, the image of the savage -Norsemen' hordes slaughtering, looting and raping their way across England has become firmly established in the popular imagination. Likewise, the ultimately triumphant resistance of King Alfred of the Saxons has become equally fixed in history as the first 'English' hero. It is therefore not surprising that this is a popular period for re-enactment, with various societies and a broad variety of approaches.

One of the most respected is *Regia Anglorum* who portray the people of Britain in the hundred years before the Norman invasion. Its 500-plus members are locally organised with each having a specified area from which they take on an accurate historic identity. While new members must conform to these identities, after three months of membership individuals are allowed to take on an identity of their own choice. It should be stressed that the vast majority of members take on the identity of ordinary 'Ceorl' rather than the high-born. Most are armed with just spear and shield with only those representing the higher born 'Thegns' carrying swords or axes.

The activities of *Regia* are extremely diverse, ranging from familiar battle re-enactments through craft displays and living history encampments. From its very foundation *Regia* dedicated itself to re-creating as accurately as possible all aspects of the period and in fact almost half its membership are involved in craft activities which are taught and exhibited at public events and at schools throughout the year. These include ship building, leather working, cooking, weaving, cabling, shoe making, iron smelting and metal forging, and even pattern welding, although members of the viewing public have to be kept well away from the last three activities for safety. These crafts are presented in period canvas tents that are 'set dressed', that is, participants live in them for the duration of a public display and so they are fully equipped for habitation.

Combat and battle is just as important with over half the membership directly involved including many of the craftsmen. Unless re-enacting a specific historic battle, combats are not choreographed but are competitive engagements where victory will go to the better side. The society tries to replicate as closely as possible the structure of a battle, the majority fighting with shield and spear, with the more experienced and higher status members wielding swords and axes. Consequently there is tremendous emphasis on training and safety, with no one permitted on the field unless passed by the National Safety Officer in the required test for the weapon they carry. The weapon itself must also be presented to the Master at Arms who ensures it is sound, that is, blunted and without

Representing the shape of things to come, these early tenth century Danish-Saxon warriors were the descendants of the victors of the bitter fifth to tenth century conflicts. Like the earlier Romano-British, the arms and armour of these Danish-Saxons reflect a mixture of cultural influences. Their riveted *spangenhelm* helmets with nasal guard and mail shirts worn over padded gambesons, reflect growing Frankish-Norman influence. However, they are still armed with traditional long bladed *Saxon seax*. English Heritage.

burred edges.

Training in all societies is not just about skill; it is also about aptitude, as in combat the object is to make a 'kill' by touching the opponent with the tip of the weapon. This impact must not injure and the recipient must 'accept' the blow and 'die'. Problems can emerge however when two or more societies come together to stage a large display–different societies allow different areas of the body to be the target: one may only allow the trunk and upper arms while another will also allow the area of the thighs. Here it is vital that, prior to combat, these matters are clearly sorted out otherwise potential disaster can strike.

1066 and the Conquest

The feudal knight dominated warfare and society throughout this period. Brought up from birth to be both a professional warrior and to assume an elevated social status, their innate mentality changed little over the centuries, but their military equipment certainly did and it is here that the first challenge to re-enactors occurs. The knights of the Crusades and Henry I fought in mail with massive iron helms adorning their heads. However, by the time Edward III crushed the French at Crecy, the descendants of the same families stood in plate armour, glad to be alongside archers drawn from the lower social strata who decimated their illustrious French cousins with the common longbow. It is inevitable that, given that neither suits of mail or plate are cheap, many societies opt for either the early or later period, but not both.

Back in 1993, a group of re-enactors sat in a pub feeling underwhelmed by their existing society's activities and standards. Rather than crying into their beer they drew up a short list of what they enjoyed, what they hated and what they wanted out of their hobby. After some eight to nine months preparation, four of this group went on to establish *Conquest* as a society, and once suitable insurance had been arranged, an initial event was organised with invited friends. A number of like-minded veteran re-enactors were rapidly attracted, each with many years of experience with groups such as *Regia Anglorum*, *The White Company*, *The English Civil War Society*, *The Vikings* and *The Company of Chivalry*, bringing with them the best practices of each. By early 1994, *Conquest*, by then with 20 or so members, was able to participate in its first public display.

The members of *Conquest* portray the period 1066–1199, essentially from the landing of William the Conqueror to the death of Richard the Lion Heart. This was the era of the Norman-Plantagenet military occupation of England and part of Wales. With never more than 20,000 soldiers to hold a country of over 3.2 million (according to the Domesday Book) it was inevitable that the Normans first became Anglo-Normans and ultimately Englishmen within three to four generations. The consequent requirement for military garrisons up and down the country, commonly of around 20 to 40 men apiece, provides a logical scenario for *Conquest* to recreate. Having said this, arms and armour inevitably underwent considerable changes during the 120 year period *Conquest* represents. To ensure an accurate representation, the society focuses on the arms and armour of three specific periods, the first being 1066–1086, the second, the civil wars between Stephen and Matilda 1135–54, and finally 1180. This allows them to narrow down the choices to be made from the various contemporary sources that cut across modern attempts to draw neat chronological divisions and instead focus on periods where the evidence indicates there was little change in clothes, armour or arms. Equally, it allows the various portrayals to demonstrate that during these decades there were obvious changes. For example in the iron mail shirt, later the *hauberk*, that first grew to the upper calf, gaining long-sleeved mail mittens along with a pair of mail hose for the legs. Subsequently, when this was found to be far too restrictive, the *hauberk* became shorter to improve mobility while shields also altered shape.

What this all means in practice is that if a member wishes to portray a knight or sergeant at all times then they must invest in effectively two full sets of mail and accoutrements, each involving an expenditure of over £1,000. Having said this, mail and weapons that were superseded by new styles and developments were far too valuable to be simply thrown away, instead they were handed down to soldiers of a lower status. Consequently, a member fully equipped as a knight for 1100 can portray a man-at-arms for the later periods with only minimal additional investment, but one is effectively socially demoted! Obviously not all elements of the Norman military machine were knights and sergeants, there being a greater number of

By the twelfth century, Norman adventurers had, carved out kingdoms as far apart as England, Southern Italy and Greece, and cemented a reputation as Christian Europe's most effective fighting force. Various styles of armour are being worn by these recreated knights, both old and new. For example, whilst the knight at the front wears a mail coif with *ventail* that completely covers the head, others have early forms of the *aventail* laced to the side and rear of the helmet. English Heritage.

common spearmen and crossbowmen. Members portraying these can take the field for as little as £200 thus enabling an entry to *Conquest* without the need for a considerable bank overdraft. In fact, *Conquest* has a policy of reinvesting all its event fees back into the Society, with provision for the purchase of the more expensive items for less affluent members.

There is also a non-combative, civilian element to *Conquest* that at present has over a dozen canvas soldier tents to enable the portrayal of the domestic life of the Norman Army. With cooking going on in the centre of the encampment, it also provides a focus for members engaged in fletching, repairing clothes and equipment, surgery, leatherwork, a forge and the many other activities associated with everyday camp life. The tented camp adds another dimension to the

group's normal display, that of a small garrison of six to ten knights and sergeants with 15 to 20 men-at-arms, crossbowmen and retainers. During the day, while the living history exhibit is ongoing, the military side provides three or four displays of archery, combat and weapons training. Training is based on the Norman *Conroi*, a unit of 15 to 30 men who trained and fought together. Commonly, a Norman army would consist of 10 to 12 *Conrois*, each senior nobleman having command of two to three. Spear and crossbowmen would then supplement this. *Conquest's* objective is to illustrate that the Normans were a professional army that trained and fought to established, though evolving, military doctrines. What this reveals to an audience is the origins of the tactics later used at Crecy and Agincourt. Norman forces drew up with half their knights dismounted to the fore; the balance remaining mounted to their rear. To either side would be small wings of bowmen to pour arrows into any attacker who would then be dispatched by the mailed fist of the knights.

The original Norman forces typically fielded knights on horseback, each knight commonly having three or four horses with a palfrey and packhorse alongside their trained battle mounts. Surprisingly for some, the knights rode short-back colts just fifteen

This typical eleventh century Man-at-Arms wears a simple short sleeved *aketon* and *spangenhelm* with nasal (nosepiece). He carries a nine-foot spear and round topped kite shield. The waist-belt that carries his sword and scabbard is typically worn at a slant as it rests over his right hip. Hannah Jenkins.

This mid-twelfth century knight wears a style of helmet that *Conquest* believes was modelled on the Phrygian cap. These are reinforced at the front to give greater protection to the head from axe and sword blows. The forward sweeping point of the helmet is designed to prevent the head protection splitting open if a blow lands directly on top of the helmet. The shield is a new 'flat-topped' design that allows the user to strike directly in front of him. Although the shield still has a boss, by this period it was more decorative than functional as the shield is attached to the arm by two sets of straps and a *guige* strap that holds the shield over the shoulder of the user thus supporting its weight. The simple repeating pattern is typical of the period; heraldic devices were not common for another 50 to 70 years. Hannah Jenkins.

hands high, rather than the stereotypical carthorse. Revealingly, during the first Crusade, foreign knights initially laughed at the small horses of the Anglo-Norman knights until they realised how little food and water these hard working steeds required.

The essential objective from the start was to establish a society that brought together people with an ethos to function as a single, dedicated team, collectively working towards a common goal. Inevitably this consciously aimed at the hardcore dedicated individual rather than those who just wanted the occasional weekend outing. Therefore, *Conquest* selectively recruits members, requiring the necessary commitment of time, effort and ethos. This has led to continuous organic growth with a desire to avoid the rapid expansion that has caused the watering down of early good intentions in other societies.

The dedication of members becomes obvious once realising the practical reality of fighting for 20 or 30 minutes during summer's heat of 85 to 90F°. Imagine

a display of combat from the period of the civil wars of Stephen and Matilda. One would stride out wearing a calf-length iron mail *hauberk* weighing in excess of 50lb's over a quilted linen *aketon* padded with wool with one's legs encompassed by a pair of iron mail hose over stout woollen hose. In addition, one's head is encompassed by a quilted cap and a mail *coif* bearing the full weight of an iron helm whilst swinging a 4lb sword with one arm and carrying a four and a half foot high wooden shield with the other. The complete harness including the weapons and shield weighs approximately 70lb's. It is thus vital that considerable quantities of water and salt are imbibed prior to such exertion, something the original Normans must equally have ensured was available.

One of the major problems confronting anybody attempting to reconstruct medieval armour or clothes is the scarcity of surviving artefacts. Clothes made from fabric or leather have long since rotted away, whilst mail and other forms of metal armour were often recycled and incorporated into later forms of armour. Ironically, due to pagan burial customs, there is a greater body of archaeological items for the early Dark Ages than afterwards. Further, as there were probably never more than around 20,000 Norman soldiers in England and as all arms and armour were subject to use and modification until they fell apart, there is little that survives. A number of *Conquest*

These two views demonstrate the working of the *ventail* on a late eleventh/early twelfth century *hauberk*. The mail *coif* covering the head is an extension of the *hauberk* and in the picture where the *ventail* is worn open it is just possible to see the edge of the padded arming cap worn beneath the coif. The *ventail* itself takes the form of a leather-backed flap that can be laced up to provide protection to the jaw and lower face. It should be stressed that this is but one interpretation of the evidence as to how the *ventail* worked. Hannah Jenkins.

members were taken into the basement of the British Museum to view its collection of eleventh and twelfth century military items, the contents of two shoe boxes! There is little more surviving across Europe. There is a mail coat attributed to St Wenceslas in Prague that may date to the tenth century, whilst in Stockholm there is another mail coat that probably came from the battlefield of Lena in 1208. There is the well-preserved sword of Fernando de la Cerda in the Monastery of Huezeas in Burgos, complete with scabbard and case, dating from 1270, whilst the Wallace Collection in London has a single German sword with a straight cross guard and brazil nut pommel dating from 1150. There is a particularly well preserved eleventh century plain straight *Spangenhelm* in Moravia, with a number of other examples in Italy. Finally, there is a single well preserved kite shield in Germany. This is almost the sum total of eleventh and twelfth century items. Thus, when it comes to historical sources for reconstructions, with so few surviving artefacts from the tenth, eleventh and twelfth century, written accounts, illuminated manuscript and carved funeral effigies are the primary sources.

Numerous illuminated manuscripts and carved monumental effigies are rich sources, partly because it was accepted practice to show the figures in biblical

This provides a side view of the *ventail* when laced-up. It also shows the distinctive profile of the Phrygian-style of helmet with nasal. As can be seen, this combination of *coif, ventail* and helmet provided a considerable degree of protection to all parts of the head and neck whilst not interfering with vision. Hannah Jenkins.

The style of *hauberk* that included an integral *coif* and *ventail* continued in use well into the twelfth century. Helmets did change and this picture provides a side view of the style of full-faced helmet that was common around 1180. This design of 'helm' developed to protect against the increased use of archery in North European warfare rather than direct blows by axe or sword, thus it still lacked protection at the back of the head. Alongside the two eye slits, the three rows of slots to aid with breathing also permitted limited vision. Hannah Jenkins.

scenes clothed and armed in the contemporary styles of the eleventh and twelfth centuries. The biblical scenes in the *Hunsterian Psalter*, dated to the 1170s, show St David in full knights armour, with over thirty other knights in various garb. Similarly, the illuminations in the *Winchester Bible*, dated to 1160–70, depict mailed soldiers in such stories as 'David and Goloath' and 'The death of Absolom'. It might be thought that the famous *Bayeux Tapestry* would be a key source, however, the arms and armour of the figures depicted is very varied and does not offer much in the way of conclusive evidence for reconstructions. Take for example the dispute over whether the eleventh century mail coat had a *ventail* or flap to guard the chin. There is no doubt that later mail shirts did, the very term *hauberk* being old German word for neck-guard. However, the *Bayeux Tapestry* illustrates somewhat enigmatic 'squares' on the chests of some soldiers. These may be early versions of the triangular

piece of mail that, with padding on the back, became the standardised *ventail* to protect the chin, or, they could be to protect the vertical neck-opening in the mail *coif*. Alternately, they may be simple squares of mail for chest re-enforcement. This particular ambiguity also appears in the mail illustrated in the tenth/eleventh century *Bible of Rhodes*, although the first unambiguous reference to the *ventail* is in the *Song of Roland* dated to around 1100. Lacking conclusive proof either way, most interpret the 'squares' as *ventails* but *Conquest* has no specific ruling and permits all variations.

Alongside manuscript illustrations are possibly the most reliable source, the three-dimensional carved funeral effigies that fill many churches. Although the iconoclasm of the Reformation and Cromwell's troops

The use of the *surcoat* had become established by the late twelfth century, often decorated with a simple pattern such as this coloured quartering. To aid movement it was cut wide at the neck and under the arms. This also marks the beginning of heraldic trappings as the coloured quartering on the *surcoat* not only matches the shield colours but is also repeated in the scarves tied around the helm. It should also be noted that the *hauberk* has now gained intrinsic mailed gloves that have a slit through the palm to facilitate ease of movement. Hannah Jenkins.

did today's researchers no favours, sufficient stone statues remain intact to provide a wealth of evidence for reconstructions. It must be born in mind that it was the accepted practice that funeral effigies were carved from life and are therefore very reliable in terms of detail. However, John Cole of *Conquest* stresses that it must be born in mind that sometimes a certain amount of 'artistic licence' has to be granted. Equally, there is a magnificent set of eleventh century carved ivory chessmen from Italy on display at the Bibliothèque Nationale in Paris that depict Italo-Norman soldiers. Both the mounted and foot figures show a wide variety of contemporary armour ranging from short lamellar coats with a leather *coif* to long sleeved mail shirts with helmet and kite shield.

In Norman armies, crossbowmen were often specialist mercenary troops who were paid more than the average man-at-arms. Here he is armed with a simple rising-pin crossbow that fired an iron-tipped bolt. He wears a simple padded Aketon over his tunic although it is just possible to make out embroidery on the cuffs of the tunic. The helmet is the old style four-piece riveted *spangenhelm* with nasal. Hannah Jenkins.

Conquest consciously chose not to represent the Norman Army as it was at Hastings. This was in fact an unusual force, specifically designed for the narrow purpose of a descent upon England. Thus it was mostly made up of high status knights and ordinary bowmen, but few men-at arms. Those men-at-arms there, were mostly mercenaries from Flanders who had a very poor reputation, the terms 'cut-throat' and 'brigand' relating specifically to these individuals. Such soldiers normally came fully equipped as part of the deal. Instead, *Conquest* represents the military forces that controlled England in subsequent years, most of whose ordinary soldiers were in fact members of the Saxon 'select' Fyrd who had become retainers under the new rulers Feudal system. The King's standing army was just his personal retine of Norman knights and archers, the latter often being on

After the Conquest, the Normans secured their domination of England with the construction of numerous castles, the garrisons of which were able to defy any challenge to Norman hegemony. These two crossbowmen under the command of a sergeant-at-arms are typical members of one of these garrisons. With little to fear from those outside, the sergeant has placed his helmet on the wall. Visible at the end of the sleeve of his *hauberk* is a form of basic hand protection that just leaves his fingers bare. Although one is decorated, both crossbowmen wear a four-piece riveted *spangenhelm* with nasal and *aketons*. The furthest crossbowman is in the act of pulling back the string of the bow by bracing the bow itself against his foot. Hannah Jenkins.

Despite their simplicity, the crossbow of the Norman period was able to propel an iron tipped bolt with sufficient force to penetrate armour. Here, a man-at-arms and a crossbowman provide aid to a sergeant-at-arms who has been shot in the shoulder by a crossbow bolt. Removal was simply a matter of brute force, as one man braces the wounded sergeant whilst the other prepares to pull the embedded bolt loose. The crossbow bolts were often buried deep in the body and were either cut loose or pushed out the other side of the body creating an additional wound. As bits of cloth and other debris was almost always driven into the wound upon impact, even if no major blood artery had been severed, subsequent infection usually proved fatal unless the wound was immediately cauterised by hot irons. Hannah Jenkins.

horseback. This force was something of a rapid reaction force that acted as a fire brigade to snuff out local uprisings. It was only in the larger field armies and local garrisons that the middle-ranking men-at-arms were common.

Taking all the contemporary evidence into account, the average man-at-arms of the 1070s was clothed in a tunic, reaching to the knee, that was sometimes split at the front and a pair of tight fitting *chausses* over baggy *braies*. Over the latter, a pair of either linen or woollen stockings or *chausses* was worn. Both contemporary illustrations and monumental effigies sometimes show leg bandages being worn over the stockings, wound spirally from the foot to just below the knee. Next came a long sleeved, thigh length, heavily padded and undecorated tunic, the *gambeson* that, like the linen shirt, was pulled on over the head. The *gambeson* was usually made from two layers of wool, leather or linen that was stuffed with an interlining of fleece, animal hair or a similar material. The thick padding of the *gambeson* meant it was often worn as armour in its own right. By the twelfth century this style of tunic was often described as an *aketon*, leading to some confusion in terminology between this and the *gambeson* as up until the thirteenth century both terms were used interchangeably. Like the *gambeson*, the *aketon* was a padded garment that covered the whole of the upper body and the arms, although it was a thinner padded garment specifically designed to be worn under mail. While mail by itself provided reasonable protection against cutting attacks, it was unable to absorb the force of a blow and the shock was transmitted straight into the wearer's body. This often caused serious internal injuries and bone fractures. The *aketon* was worn under the mail to absorb some of this shock. It also prevented the mail links from chaffing the wearer's skin.

The primary item of armour was the mail shirt or *hauberk*, which like the preceding items was pulled on

This interior of a late twelfth century tent gives an idea of the few home comforts life on campaign had to offer. There is rush matting on the floor whilst the simple wooden pallet the soldier slept on is held together with wooden pegs thus allowing the pallet to be rapidly disassembled for transport. The wooden chest at the back of the tent contains clothes along with other few personal items and valuables. Given the full-face helm on the right and the selection of swords and a mace on the pallet, the occupant of this tent may be a knight.
Hannah Jenkins.

over the head. At the time of the Conquest, *hauberks* were knee length with short or elbow-length sleeves. For those who were mounted, mostly knights, the skirt of the *hauberk* was slit at front and rear to facilitate movement in the saddle and to ensure the mail hung over the thighs. For the majority of men-at-arms who fought on foot, the skirt of the *hauberk* had side vents instead. Either as an extension of the *hauberk* or occasionally as a separate item, a padded mail *coif* covered the head. Under the mail *coif* was the arming cap, a padded bonnet that provided the same protective function as the *Aketon*. Some arming caps also incorporated a small hemispherical skullcap made of iron. This was laced or riveted to the outside of the arming cap and was often the only head protection worn by poorer men-at-arms. However the junction of the neck and shoulders was vulnerable to attacks from above. Evidence from medieval war graves and period illustrations show that this area was a prime target. The development of a separate *coif* by the thirteenth century could have been a response to this. It effectively provides an extra layer of protection over the top of the wearer's torso. Early forms of *coifs* had the *ventail* laced or buckled to its side. Reconstructed *coifs* are generally made from very fine mail and weigh 4kg. The only other piece of armour at this time, but only worn by a few senior knights, were mail *chausses*

strapped to the front of the leg and laced at the rear and additional mail worn on the forearms.

Most ordinary men-at-arms wore the somewhat old-fashioned *spangenhelm* made from four pieces of iron attached by riveted strips running down the joints, with the distinctive nasal or nose-guard. Whilst common amongst the knights, a few men-at-arms wore the newer conical helmets beaten out from a single piece of metal. Although the nasal or nose-guard was usually a separate piece riveted to the brow-band, a few had the nose-guard forged in one with the helmet. Made from a single piece of metal, these helmets provided far greater protection than the earlier riveted *spangenhelm*. However, given the time involved in making them in this way, only a wealthy knight could afford such an item. Although none have survived with a lining, it is almost certain all helmets were lined, particularly as the few surviving items have holes for rivets whose only logical function could be to attach a lining. The most probable lining would have been coarse cloth or felt that was stuffed and quilted, being stitched to the brim.

To complete the men-at-arms equipage was the standard kite-shaped shield, used by both cavalry and infantry. Reproductions of shields are generally made from laminations of plywood that are soaked in water and moulded to form a curve across its lateral surface. The curve was designed to help deflect blows away from the shield. A small section of padding was attached to the back of the shield to protect the wearer's forearm from the impact of heavy blows on the shield. The shield had two leather straps called '*enarmes*' riveted to its back to loop the user's arm through. Although these early style shields had a boss, these were purely ornamental and became part of the general decorative pattern painted onto the face of the shield. These patterns were the forerunners of the later twelfth century heraldic symbols.

In keeping with contemporary evidence, most of *Conquest*'s men-at-arms are just armed with a spear, few soldiers in the eleventh century below the rank of knight having a sword. Those that do, have the familiar straight-bladed, double-edged sword of 31in in length. As these were wielded in one hand, the hilts were short with a simple straight crossguard and the long established tea-cosy or brazil nut shaped pommel. The leather covered wooden scabbard was slung from a waistbelt.

By the mid-twelfth century little had changed. There are more references to the *aketon*, although the term *gambeson* was still almost as common. This garment was now of a tighter fit, heavier and reached to the knees. The mail *hauberk* was of similar length with elbow, if not full length sleeves. This change was primarily due to practical experience in the Crusades that had caused the *gambeson* to become arrow proof and consequently more padded. Helmets and shields had changed little, although whilst spears were still the main weapon, swords were becoming far more common amongst the ordinary men-at-arms. Although these swords had in general changed little, as the twelfth century progressed a new style of blade evolved that was slightly shorter and tapered towards its tip.

The big change came at the end of the twelfth century as the ongoing influence of the Crusades continued to make itself felt. The *Assize of Arms* of Henry II still lists mostly knee length, long sleeved padded *gambesons* with mail *hauberk* as the common form of armour. Added to this though were mail hose and mittens as the knight became fully armoured. The illumination of Joshua in the *Winchester Bible* show several figures with mail mittens that leave the fingers exposed. Once the hand was fully enclosed in mail, leather or cloth, palms had to be stitched on to allow a firm grip to be retained on spear or shield. Equally, helmets were becoming fully enclosed with more padding, under which a quilted cap was becoming common. More cylindrical in shape with just two slits for the eyes and pierced with holes or slots for ventilation, this helmet was the forerunner of the thirteenth century great helm.

Visually, the most obvious innovation was a new garment, the *surcoat*, which was worn over the mail *hauberk*. Again, this was a consequence of the Crusades where it had proved necessary to keep the rays of the sun from so heating the iron rings of the mail as to make it impossibly hot to wear. The clothes of the Saracens probably influenced its long flowing style. Early *surcoats* are depicted as 'over-tunics' with long sleeves and full-length cuffs. The sleeves quickly vanished, probably due to their impracticability on the battlefield. Illuminations and monumental effigies show the *surcoat* drawn tight around the waist by a belt of some design. Although pictures show these *surcoats* as white to begin with, albeit often with a contrasting coloured lining, as heraldry began to evolve it became an obvious garment, alongside the shield, to display heraldic arms.

Although kite-shaped shields remained common, the practice of cutting the top edge flat was spreading. This permitted the mounted knight and men-at-arms to see over its top rather than having to move the shield to one side thus exposing themselves. There is a well-preserved specimen of such, dated to the late twelfth century, in the Swiss National Museum in Zurich. However, the infantry were losing their shields, for whilst spears were still common in illuminations and lists of arms, there was a distinct move towards polearms. There is a suggestion that the morale of the infantry was in decline as they were becoming less willing to stand up to the charge of the more heavily mailed knights. Consequently the traditional shield wall was giving way to the more familiar mix of bowmen mixed with soldiers armed with polearms.

Finally, although it was to be the first half of the thirteenth century that witnessed a move away from mail towards plate, research has revealed there were attempts to strengthen mail from as early as the late twelfth century. However, it was in the fourteenth century that there was the most rapid evolution in armour. During this period supplementary forms of protection were developed in a haphazard fashion but at the expense of mobility. These developments persisted until the age of full plate armour that began in the early fifteenth century.

Wars of the Roses

Just as plate armour was being perfected, so the age of gunpowder and firearms truly dawned, ultimately rendering all armour worthless. As the fifteenth century progressed, the once almighty knight came to be confronted by disciplined and ever better equipped professional infantry armed with various weapons capable of crushing and piercing even the finest German or Italian armour. Various types of polearms – halberts, bills and poll-axes–could both crack plate and drag even the most accomplished horseman from his saddle. Crossbows and longbows had already established that the appropriate bolt or arrowhead could piece plate in most circumstances and gunpowder completed the process of demonstrating the ultimate vulnerability of plate. The Swiss demonstrated that the pike, if utilised in the appropriate tactical fashion, could overcome the armoured warrior and by the mid-fifteenth century the handgun and cannon were beginning to establish what would ultimately come to be their total dominance of the battlefield by the seventeenth century.

The prestige already attached to cannon was signalled by the significant sums of money being made by many master gunners who were retained by any self-respecting grandee. This was despite the fact that on the battlefield the early fieldpieces were only capable of causing significant casualties when ranged against large bodies of tightly packed men. However, even before the fifteenth century had begun, cannon were influencing how fixed defences were built. In Southampton, the city walls were rebuilt with gun 'loops', a purpose built gun 'tower' and the city equipped with ordnance. By 1460, even this was considered inadequate as the city complained that the walls were 'so feeble that they may not resist against any gun shot'. By the late fifteenth century, whilst the heavier guns were useful in defending castles, in England at least, they were still not playing a significant role in taking them due to the difficulty of transport. Despite this, an indication of what was to come in England came in 1463 when even the imposing walls of Bamburgh Castle fell to a fierce artillery bombardment by the cannon of the Earl of Warwick.

Whilst fully armoured knights and men-at-arms still appeared, particularly in the French Army, these various developments meant that the common foot soldier could now overcome their social superiors with ease. Consequently, the chivalric elite began to ape their social inferiors by adopting their weapons and gradually shedding their armour and abandoning concepts of armies based on social rank and status. In 1437, Charles VII of France began raising a more 'national' and 'professional' army, increasingly dominated by infantry and by his *Ordonnance de la Gendarmerie*, a move matched by Burgundy. For the Burgundian Army, the *Ordinance of Abbeville* of 1471 removed the distinction between Chevalier Baronets, Chevalier Bacheleurs and Ecuyères, all men-at-arms being henceforth paid the same regardless of social status. Thus began the gradual process by which the once distinct body of armoured knights transformed into a professional officer corps and came to operate almost as sub-contractors, raising 'companies' with royal commissions on behalf of the 'national' monarch.

As the first national armies began to emerge, so did the concept of identifying uniforms. Whilst the ancient Romans could be said to have worn an identifiable 'uniform' as such, with legions and possibly cohorts displaying their particular unit designation, the collapse of Roman power in the West had ended all such uniformity. The next 1000 years could be termed 'the age of the warrior', be it the Viking berserker or feudal knight. The very concept of warrior denotes individualism and, whilst they evolved a complex iconography of personal identification that is feudal heraldry, there was very little to suggest an identifiable visual corporate identification other than

The series of dynastic conflicts collectively known as the Wars of the Roses represent a period of military transition between the age of plate armour and the longbow, and the age of gunpowder. However, many battles quickly descended into vicious mêlée where the polearm continued to hold sway. The very wide variety of armour and protective clothing commonly worn during the conflict is represented here by members of the *Stafford Household*, including various styles of sallet, basinet, jack and white harness. English Heritage.

the flying of specific standards. The closest feudal armies came to common identification in clothes was the use of coloured badges or very basic livery jackets worn over armour or ordinary clothes. If there were any common motifs of identification they were invariably religious, for example the insignia of the Knights Templars and other similar symbols associated with the crusades. However, these were strictly limited to the knights and their men-at-arms, the peasant levies being left to simply wear their own clothes. It was thus the fourteenth and fifteenth centuries that witnessed the first move towards common 'uniform' items in 'national' field armies. At Agincourt, many of King Henry's common soldiers were recorded as wearing the cross of St George, and in Scotland, from the mid-fourteenth century, soldiers had been ordered

to wear a white cross of St Andrew. Equally, the badge of the particular aristocratic household who had raised a body of troops, be it for their own purposes or as part of the monarch's army became the norm. The records for Edward IV's 1475 invasion of France list the main lords who had been indentured to provide soldiers alongside their badges, their soldiers wearing white jackets with the red cross of St George and the respective lord's badge.

The very name 'Wars of the Roses', although anachronistic in itself, indicates how visual identification was becoming recognised and these conflicts witnessed a considerable evolution in this aspect as the respective grandees ensured their particular household's symbol was prominently displayed. More accurately described as liveries, coats, tunics or just sewn-on badges displayed each lord's coat of arms and/or the colour of his principle charge. These were no longer dominated by the rules of heraldry. Hence, although the tinctures of the Percy arms were azure, that household's troops wore a livery of russet, yellow and orange, with the Percy's blue lion rampant worn on their shoulder. Prior to the second battle of St Albans in February 1461, the commentator Pseudo-Gregory described Queen Margaret's men as wearing a basic uniform that included each

Here, members of the *White Company* provide a close-up view of soldiers preparing to close with polearms. Although the concept of uniform was still very much in its infancy, there is a commonality of clothing and equipment. All wore some form of helmet, mostly one or other style of *sallet*, although the soldier in the centre wears a Kettle Hat. Most wear some type of protective armour for the body, albeit just a plate armour breastplate. The soldier wearing the painted *sallet* on the right and the soldier wearing the Kettle hat in the centre both wear a *bevor* (a plate armour gorget protecting the throat and neck). Both are armed with sword and buckler, the latter being a small shield usually made from iron. Gillian Perry.

Household's particular livery but also a common army wide badge of Prince Edward's ostrich feathers superimposed on a 'bend' (posibly a cloth sash) of crimson and black (It is important to sound a note of caution in regard to the term 'livery' as it could sometimes just mean 'issued'. There is reference to 'liveries' of spoons, firewood and shoes, thus the context of any contemporary quote is crucial.) As a result, with the Wars' conclusion, England acquired its first truly uniformed body of regular troops in the guise of Henry VII's Yeomen of the Guard. Henceforth, they wore the white and green Tudor livery in vertical stripes with a red rose within a vine wreath on both the chest and back. When his son, Henry VIII, led an army to France in 1513, many common soldiers were issued a basic white coat bearing the cross of St George, a uniform item already so well established that the term 'white-coat' had already become almost interchangeable with the word 'soldier' in contemporary England.

In England this transformation of warfare had already begun to commence with the last of the English armies that fought in France before their expulsion in the late 1440s. The next 50 years found these veterans participating in a series of dynastic and aristocratic conflicts collectively know as the Wars of the Roses, which witnessed the progressive impact of these changes. If the longbow and poleaxe dominated the field of the First Battle of St Albans in 1455, the professional Landsknechts of the luckless Captain Martin Schwarz at the Battle of Stoke in 1487 included hundreds of men armed with arquebuses. The chronicler Jean Molinet described Schwarz's men as 'loaded with…artillery'. Equally, in 1475 the splendid train of artillery, both field and siege pieces, taken to France by Edward IV was sufficiently impressive that it drew comments from contemporaries. The significant expansion of the royal ordnance department that was responsible for assembling these guns illustrates how the Wars of the Roses ensured a new generation of professional English officers were kept abreast of rapidly evolving military technology.

Today, this crucial and colourful period of English history is brought to life by one of Britain's finest living history groups, *The White Company*. When, in 1983, Clive Bartlett founded *The White Company* there were already various medieval societies but none specialised in the period known as The Wars of the Roses (1455–87). One of the fundamental motivations was to try and dispel some of the myths surrounding this period. Thus the objective was to create a society that offered a credible and accurate portrayal of the everyday life of the mid-fifteenth century for education and entertainment, but also to encourage research into the period. The ultimate goal then, as it very much remains, being to push back the bounds of

knowledge of life in the fifteenth century. Initially, the *Company* concentrated on the military side, but quite quickly activities expanded into the numerous civilian aspects of the age and the authenticity demands of living history.

The *White Company* averages around 100 members who pride themselves on being able to portray a broad span of ordinary fifteenth century medieval life, although the prime focus is on Edward IV's reign, and in particular 1468–71 (a period that encompasses the final years of Edward IV's first reign, the restoration of Henry VI and finally Edward's dramatic campaign to reclaim the throne). It is therefore ironic that the title 'The White Company' refers to a fourteenth century body of English mercenaries who fought in Italy under the leadership of the famous Condottieri, Sir John Hawkwood. As the society evolved, the contradictions and confusion inherent in the name led

As in all wars, much of a soldier's time was spent in garrison and on guard. On the right of this picture, a captain of the King's Household checks on his men. The Captain wears a good quality visored *sallet*, mail *standard*, breastplate and full arm harness. Over this he is wearing his livery of a jacket of murrey and blue with the white rose on a Sun with streamers. Both the captain and soldier are armed with sword and buckler. Dave Key.

This close-up of the soldier reveals the detail of the painted linen Pennon bearing the badges of Edward IV: a White Rose on a 'Sunne with Stremys' (Warkworth's Chronicle) and a White Rose. The soldier wears civilian clothing with a visored *sallet* and breastplate. By his side hangs a sword and buckler. It is unclear if the bearers of pennons received extra wages, but Standard and Banner bearers were paid twice the rate of other soldiers. Dave Key.

Many soldiers were actually indentured and were consequently issued their arms and equipment. Reflecting the common items of equipment worn by ordinary soldiers, the recently arrayed archer on the left has been issued a simple open-faced Sallet and Jack. The difference between his newly issued items that are clean and shiny and the dull and pitted condition of armour worn by the experienced campaigner he is talking is obvious.
Dave Key.

to discussions about changing it. However, many who worked with the group advised against this as they had established something of a 'brand name' for excellence under this name, so it was kept but the dates '1450–1485' were added to clarify things somewhat.

When the *Company* was originally established it was organised into 'Households', such as example, Sir John Howards, the Oxford Household, the Stafford Household, etc., in an attempt to reflect contemporary practice. However by 1989 it had become clear that this structure was unable to meet either the needs or the aims of the society, so the *Company* was fundamentally restructured. Today all members simply belong to *The White Company* with, for most military and domestic scenarios, members portraying part of the extended Household of Edward IV, although this is tailored to meet the specific needs of each event.

Members take on a role appropriate to each scenario, for example one day a retained archer in Edward's Household, next a panel painter belonging to the Gild of Saynte Luke, then a Household Officer ensuring a formal meal is correctly served, each activity operating under the guidance of the society's Fifteenth Century Officers: the Captain, Master of Mysteries and Steward. To ensure that standards of equipment are maintained and constantly improved, members use the Company Handbook and Standards, many of which have become *de facto* standards for much fifteenth century re-enactment. This has drawn on the surviving contemporary sources to provide provenances for reconstructions, for which the Society is relatively well served both in documentation and artefacts.

For the military, the vast majority of ordinary troops in the mid-fifteenth century were low status archers (up to 80 per cent) and men-at-arms, often simply referred to either as soldiers or 'spears' (the term 'billmen' does not seem to appear in the historical record until the mid-sixteenth century). The Paston letters give a classic description of these men, 'jakked and saletted redy for were', a description reinforced by the Venetian ambassador to England, Dominic Mancini, who, in 1483, described the northern soldiers brought to London by Richard of Gloucester as there being: '...hardly any without a helmet and none without bows and arrows. Their bows and arrows are thicker and longer than those used by other nations, just as their bodies are stronger than other peoples, for they seem to have hands and arms of iron. The range of their bows is no less than our arbalests [crossbows]. There hangs by the side of each a sword no less long than ours but heavy and thick as well. An iron buckler accompanies the sword. They do not wear any metal armour, except for the better sort who have breastplates and some with full harness. Indeed the common soldiery has more comfortable tunics [Jacks] that reach below the loins and are stuffed with tow or some other soft material. They say that the softer the tunics the better do they withstand the blows of arrows and swords.'

These 'common' soldiers wore everyday clothing underneath their armour, clothing that included a

The English soldier was renowned not only for his fighting skills but also his drunken behaviour and love of gambling. Here soldiers of the King's Household gamble away their pay playing with a set of the new playing cards imported from Germany. Behind the two seated soldiers, the bowman, whose longbow is in its protective cover, is wearing an ordinary Jack and civilian cloth hat. Dave Key.

simple linen shirt and 'breeches' (which resembled close fitting shorts with a pouch at the front for 'comfort'). Over these were worn full-length hose with joined leggings (single leg hose were still being worn by the lowest levels of society), for the ordinary soldier made from various types of woollen cloth including coarse twill kersey or worsted. These could be lined in linen and reached the hip where they were attached to the doublet, or for the 'better sort' an arming doublet, by points (laces). For most soldiers the outfit was completed by a pair of low ankle boots made from tanned cattle hide that buckled at the ankle.

For many, much of their clothing was supplied as 'livery', similarly the obligation to provide the armour and weapons would fall upon the men, or civic authorities, who had signed indentures to provide the soldiers. For example, in 1475 Edmund Paston committed to supply himself and three archers for Richard of Gloucester's contingent of Edward IV's invasion of France. For towns, the mayor and aldermen, depending upon their position, were obliged to equip set numbers of soldiers when required.

The surviving *Coventry Leet Book* records the sets of equipment provided by each civic officer: in 1450 the city equipped the 40-strong City Watch with *Jacks*, *Sallets* and *Poleaxes* or *Glaives*. Five years later, just

prior to the First Battle of St Albans, the city again issued *Jacks* and *Sallets* to their 100-strong force, but this time bows and arrows replaced the polearms, possibly reflecting the differing needs of a city watch and an army in the field. In the 1480s, Sir John Howard equipped the majority of his soldiers with Sallet, Brigandine and an assortment of other pieces of mail and plate armour (particularly Standards and mail sleeves). All of these records fit well with Burgundian ordinances for 1472 (English soldiers formed an essential part of the Burgundian archery force). This required archers to have a *Brigandine* or padded *Jack*, arm reinforcement, a *Sallet*, a *Gorgerin* (this was some form of protection to the throat, either a mail Standard or a metal gorget *Bevor*), a long dagger, a

Whilst the longbow still remained the predominate projectile weapon at the end of the fifteenth century, the handgun was becoming a more common sight on the battlefield. As can be seen, the weapon of this veteran hand-gunner is an arquebus with a simple matchlock trigger system, a firing mechanism that would remain little changed for over two hundred years. Whilst lead musket balls could not penetrate plate armour, iron balls could and did, thus effectively signalling the end of armour. Judging from the condition of his Kettle Hat, he has been in the field for some time. Gillian Perry.

lead hammer and a sheaf of 30 arrows.

Contemporary illustrations, such as the archers illustrated in Memlinc's *Reliquary of St Ursula*, and both the archers and men-at-arms illustrated in the *Beachamp Chronicles* support the written evidence. The elite household archers of Charles VII of France (the 'Scots Archers') are shown wearing *Sallets*, short sleeved *Brigandines* over full arm harness and with full leg harness. Interestingly the records reveal these archers were initially equipped with *Brigandines* (as depicted in contemporary illustrations), but these were soon replaced by *Jacks*, as they were considered a better defence, although this was apparently not a popular decision with the archers. This was the ultimate in archers' armour as it provided an effective

This front and back view shows a well-arrayed Man-at-Arms in full harness. This Italian export harness is typical of the style of armour popular in England during the Wars of the Roses. It provided the ultimate in protection against blows from polearms and swords combined with mobility. The visored *sallet* is here worn open, although in combat it would be dropped so as to provide complete protection to face and neck in conjunction with the *bevor*. On the rear view it is possible to see the difference in size between the *pauldrons* on the left and right shoulders. Gillian Perry.

compromise between protection and the ability to accurately shoot their bow.

Researching the reconstruction of a *Sallet* presents few difficulties given the survival of numerous items in collections throughout Britain and the Continent. The issue is rather one of identifying which surviving *Sallets* represent the average 'English' *Sallet* and which the exception, that is, higher status. As with so many other surviving artefacts from any age, there is always the question as to why a particular item has survived, and the answer is often that it belonged to a high status owner. Apart from obvious intrinsic evidence as regards the craftsmanship and quality of the item, recourse must be made to contemporary illustrations in an attempt to identify the types of design most

often associated with the common soldier in England.

Fortunately, a considerable number of surviving *Sallets* in British collections are of very similar design suggesting a broad commonality, and these further match those illustrated in contemporary pictures such as those in the *Beauchamp Chronicles*. These suggest the English armourers copied the German style of *Sallet* that had evolved from a combination of the native German *Kettle Hat* and the Franco-Burgundian version of the Italian *celata* (an open faced *Bascinet* style helmet with a conical skull enclosing the sides of the face). This was generally larger and deeper than the previous styles, with a long tail sloping downwards at the rear. The simplest *Sallets* were open faced, although some had a small half-visor that formed a sight between its upper edge and the outwardly turned edge of the helmet itself, while others had a full visor, or they could be made in a single piece with a slit for the eyes. Original *Sallets* were hammered out or 'raised' from a single piece of metal and then ground to shape. This both made them inherently very strong and produced a fine, glancing surface that could deflect most angled blows from bladed weapons such as swords and polearms. There are armourers today who can do this, although such magnificent pieces can cost in excess of £2,400. Given such costs, many modern reconstructions are made from two pieces of metal that are welded together, although even these retail in excess of £400 once ground to shape.

For men-at-arms, the *Sallet* was normally worn with a *Bevor*, a chin-shaped piece of plate armour that covered the front of the face, normally to just below or just above the nose. This incorporated one or more gorget plates, thus providing comprehensive defence to the lower half of the face. On German-style *Bevors* these armour plates were invariably pointed and extended over the top of any breastplate that was worn. Another common style of helmet was the *Kettle Hat*. This was essentially a broad brimmed visorless helmet that often had a slight point to the top and a deep bowl, the tail section of the brim usually being wider and longer than the brow. There is evidence, including the *Beauchamp Chronicles*, that these, like some *Sallets*, could be cloth-covered and richly decorated, and/or using large decorative rivets to attach the lining. As with any age, older styles of helmet also continued in use, such as *Bascinets*.

This man-at-arms wears a German style harness, the fluted surface of which was to deflect blows. Also, rather than a plate armour gorget *bevor* to protect the throat, this soldier wears a mail *standard* that can be seen tied by leather laces to the *pauldrons*. Gillian Perry.

Possibly the most evocative and debated item of late medieval clothing is the *Jack*, a cloth body armour made either from multiple layers of linen, and fustian, or stuffed, for example with tow. The thickness of the panels could vary, with less padding on the back and arms than the front. Although there are some surviving items labelled as *Jacks*, for example there is one in a Yorkshire collection said to be from the Battle of Towton, there is some doubt as to their precise provenance given *Jacks* continued in use well into the mid-sixteenth century. More reliable as sources for reconstruction are the various contemporary documents describing the composition of *Jacks*. Considerable detail is provided in the *Ordinances* of Louis XI of France: 'And first they must have for the said Jacks, 30, or at least 25 folds of cloth and a stag's skin; those of 30, with the stag's skin, being the best cloth that as been worn and rendered flexible, is best for this purpose, and these Jacks should be made in four quarters. The sleeves should be as strong as the body, with the exception of the leather, and the arm-hole of the sleeve must be large, which arm-hole should be placed near the collar, not on the bone of the shoulder, that it may be broad under the armpit and full under the arm, sufficiently ample and large on the sides below. The collar should be like the rest of the Jack, but not too high behind, to allow room for

This front and back view demonstrates how a Man-at-Arms required assistance when arming. Here the *rarebrace* of the arm harness is being attached by strong waxed cord or 'points' to the padded arming doublet. In the front view it is possible to see how the lower half of the breastplate is strengthened by a *plackart*. Philipp Elliot-Wright.

the sallet. This Jack should be laced in front, and under the opening must be a hanging piece [porte piece] of the same strength as the Jack itself. Thus the Jack will be secure and easy, provided that there be a doublet [pourpoint] without sleeves or collar, of two folds of cloth, that shall be only four fingers broad on the shoulder; to which doublet shall be attached the chausses. Thus shall the wearer float, as it were, within his jack and be at his ease; for never have been seen half a dozen men killed by stabs or arrow wounds in such Jacks, particularly if they be troops accustomed to fighting.'

The *Household Accounts of Sir John Howard* include for January 1464 a similar description of a 'dobelete of fense'. This also refers to the body of the *Jack* being cut from four panels, the front having 23 'folds' of linen and fustian, the back twenty-one and the arms nine. Two Scottish Acts of Parliament, for 1456 and 1481 respectively, stress long sleeves and that the

bottom hem should either reach the top of the leg harness if worn, or cover the upper leg if it was not. These written descriptions are supported by contemporary illustrations, such as, the Swiss *Schilling* chronicles showing Burgundian archers (quite possibly English mercenaries) wearing padded armour with short puffed sleeves, high collars and a short scalloped-edged skirt. All are well tailored, with a clear waist. Illustrations by Memlinc, a Flemish source of the 1470s and 80s, show similar padded garments, one with full length sleeves with a short puffed sleeve-head, another with long sleeves. Visible quilting shows vertically stitched rows, diagonal cross-stitching and knotting. The illustrations also reveal that the common soldier would often supplement the protection of the *Jack* with a steel cuirass, along with other pieces of mail or plate armour such as leg and arm harness.

The construction of another common body armour, the *Brigandine*, also gives cause for debate. This was cloth covered armour made by riveting rows of overlapping tinned iron plates through a layer of canvas and an outer layer of cloth, often fustian or velvet. As with the *Jack*, although several *Brigandines* have survived, their precise dating is unclear, *Brigandines* being in use through to the mid-sixteenth

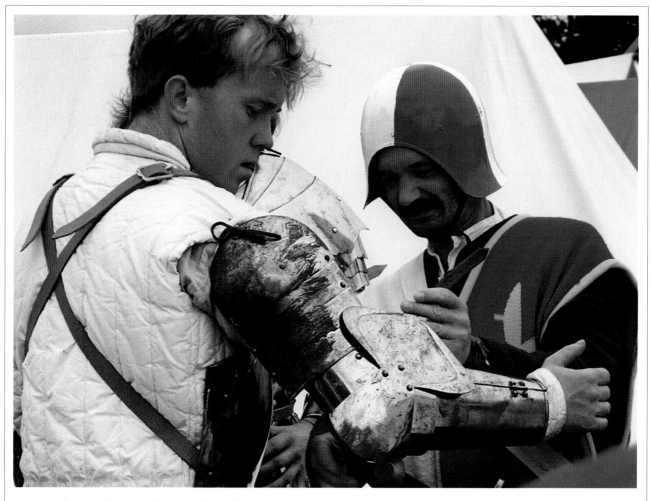

century. At one time the Tower of London stored literally thousands of such items. Unfortunately most, some 6,000 plus, were issued in the 1580s to soldiers departing to fight the Spanish in Holland. Realising that fifteenth century *Brigandines* would be utterly useless against Spanish musket balls, the whole lot was thrown overboard into the English Channel as a useless encumbrance. A similar fate awaited the thousands of Bills stored in the Tower when they were issued to soldiers departing for Ireland a few years later, the lot being reputedly sold off to Irish farmers. Utilising the few *Brigandines* that have survived, particularly one in Italy, the riveting had a characteristic series of triangular groupings of three rivets. The surviving examples demonstrate the dangers of relying solely on 'survivals' as all are front opening, buckled across with five or more straps, with no sleeves or internal lining, and reach the hips, whilst illustrations also show side openings and sleeves. Like those wearing *Jacks*, the body protection offered by the *Brigandine* was supplemented by additional items of mail or plate armour.

To ensure identification, the common soldier was usually issued as 'livery' a jacket to wear over their body armour. Contemporary illustrations, such as in *Froissart* and the *Beauchamp Chronicles*, show the most common as being a sleeveless 'waistcoat-style' jacket. Written sources suggest these were made from woollen cloth, and also show the Captains being issued with better quality Jackets and 'gowns', often made from silk. For Edward IV's soldiers, accounts record the issue of Jackets of blue and murrey cloth with white rose badges (simple, cheap, mass produced items with the appropriate household design either painted and/or embroidered on). These badges, together with Standards, Banners and Pennons, were probably the most important means of identification in battle and the source of much of the confusion, as at Barnet in 1471 where the Earl of Oxford's Star with Streamers was mistaken in the fog for Edward's Sun with Streamers.

Whilst the vast majority of common soldiery wore *Sallets, Jacks, Brigandines* and, if fortunate, a selection of mail and plate armour to protect arms and legs, those of a higher social status wore harness, commonly referred to as '*White Harness*' due to the highly polished surface. By the mid-fifteenth century, plate armour had come of age, almost entirely superseding mail. The reconstruction of a complete plate armour harness is possibly one of the most challenging of all for the re-enactor. The fundamental advantage of plate armour is that it offered the same, if not better,

Here several well-arrayed Men-at-Arms in White Harness muster by a standard of Saint George outside the walls of Dover Castle. Visible are several different styles of *sallet* and a pole-axe, the latter being the preferred weapon of men-at-arms with its combination of axe-head, hammer and spike for thrusting. Gillian Perry.

level of protection that mail did at less weight and with far more mobility. Whilst the weight of a mail hauberk rested mainly on the shoulders, plate armour was attached to the body thus distributing the weight in a balanced way. This permitted great agility, both on horseback and on foot, and permitted a knight or man-at-arms to fight for far longer. Just how much agility was permitted is reflected in a fifteenth century illustration of a knight turning a cartwheel in full plate armour. Unlike Hollywood, which confuses heavy jousting armour for battle armour, thus stereo-typing knights as having to be hauled into the saddle by a crane, *Froissart* relates how Sir John Assueton leaped fully armoured onto his war-horse. Dismounting was equally straightforward, Olivier de la Marche writing in 1446 relates how Galliot de Balthasin leaped fully armoured from his saddle 'as though he had on a pourpoint only'. There are even accounts, albeit somewhat exaggerated, of fully armoured knights being pulled safely from rivers and lakes with the assistance of just one or two squires.

The total average weight of late fifteenth century armour was around 52lbs, this being evenly distributed on the body. The knight would first put on a well-padded, linen arming doublet, to which much of the mail and plate was now attached. With the assistance of his squire, gussets of mail were first tied onto the arming doublet and hose with strong waxed cord, any surplus cord being cut off. Next, a collar of mail was put on, either buckled or buttoned at the side or rear. The first stage was completed by mail 'shorts' being worn over the hose, these being attached with points. All this mail came to a total weight of between 15–20lbs. Now the plate armour was attached from the bottom up. First were the metal plate shoes or *sabetons*. Next the *greaves* were put on enclosing the calf of the leg, these being hinged vertically down the outside. The *cuisse* (thigh piece) and *poleyn* (knee piece) completed the lower half, these being strapped against the leg and probably attached to the top of the hose at the thigh by laces. The leg armour totalled around 6lbs. Next came the back and breastplates that were buckled down the right hand side and included an attached skirt piece or *fauld*. This was by far the heaviest piece of plate weighing in excess of 12–13lbs.

To this was added the *tassets* to protect the groin area weighing about 2lbs. The arm and shoulder pieces were now laced to the arming doublet at the shoulder and buckled around the arms in four major parts. The *pauldron* protected the shoulder, the *rarebrace* the upper arm, the *couter* the elbow and the *vambrace* the forearm. As it wielded the sword, mace, or other weapon, the armour of the right arm was slightly lighter than that of the left or reigns arm. The additional weight for the left arm was due to the size of the *couter* being increased in size to provide additional protection, the shield having been abandoned. Thus the plate of the left arm weighed around 3lbs, that of the right around 2lbs. 8oz. The two final pieces of armour were the *Bevor* to protect the neck, weighing as little as 9oz, and the helmet, which depending on type, came in at a more substantial 6–7lbs. To complete the process for battle' a coat was worn over the armour bearing either the wearer's own arms or that of his lord's livery, vital if the knight was to be identified in close combat by his friends.

Various re-enactors have confirmed contemporary accounts that the main problem with all this could be the helmet, which if closed, lacked ventilation and close range visibility. Whilst closed helmets offered more protection, by the late fifteenth century most knights and men-at-arms preferred open helmets, sometimes even leaving aside lower face plates regardless of the increased risk of fatal injury. The calculation was based on the empirical experience that with a helmet's visor closed they were far more likely to be taken down by two or three less well armoured attackers coming in from different angles.

Whilst plate armour was a major technological advance in protection, the knight's weaponry had changed little from previous centuries, although their method of fighting certainly had. When mounted, the sword, axe and mace predominated, although most English knights and men-at-arms fought on foot with poll-axes ('poll' means head), a combination weapon of axe, hammer and spike standing roughly at man-height and often with a rondel to protect the hand about halfway up the shaft. The poll-axe was an extremely effective weapon capable of delivering terrific crushing, cutting and puncturing blows.

Most plate armour of the fifteenth century has been classified by modern collectors in certain 'styles' that all too often have neither any basis in the contemporary period nor are appropriate to their actual place of manufacture. The highest quality armour in use in England by the most experienced and richest soldiers, was the plain, workman-like,

'Milanese'. The lighter, richly decorated and fluted German, or 'Gothic', harness does not appear to have been common in England until the very end of the century. Rather, the most popular style of harness worn by the common and middling sort was based on a variety of types, styles and qualities of armour, often worn in multiple layers, instead of the complete harness of the wealthy. This had the generic term of 'Flemish' armour, apparently based on the 'Italian export' style and something of a cross between the 'Milanese' and 'German' styles. To illustrate just how mixed were styles, at French centres of manufacture at Tours and Lyons most of the armourers working for the French monarch were Italians, whilst in England, German craftsmen commonly worked alongside their English brethren.

Regardless of style, very few could actually afford such armour, thus restricting the ownership of White Harness to wealthy merchants and the landed classes. Equally, to keep the harness clean and polished, a daily task in the field, it required the employment of various lackeys. Even then, only the most affluent knight could afford to continually upgrade their harness to reflect the most recent styles. Rather, many were lucky enough to inherit armour, although this ensured many pieces of older armour, some of it modified, was mixed with more recent items. Certainly by the 1440s, English wills and inventories commonly mentioned imported armours, particularly from Lombardy. Soldiers were normally issued their harness, it being common for the wealthier landed magnates having much in storage for their Household, for example Sir Thomas Burgh. This though again contributed to many older pieces remaining a common sight on the field of combat.

A pertinent comment by Mark Griffin of the *White Company* on modern reconstructions of harness is that there are many bad copies of good armour, but few good copies of mediocre. The fundamental problem in deciding what is the appropriate style to reflect the commoner sort of harness for modern reconstruction's is the shortage of surviving pieces that can be conclusively dated to the mid- or late-fifteenth century. The Tower of London, which ought to have been the major source either stored it until it rusted away or long ago sold most of the surviving harness for scrap metal. Equally, much of the harness that has survived was at some point in its career re-used and subject to modification, leaving doubt as to its original style or when it was re-styled. Needless to say, of the armour that has survived, very few pieces can be identified as that used by the common soldier. More reliable, but surprisingly often overlooked, are the numerous monumental brasses and alabaster effigies dating from the fifteenth century that grace many English churches. In considerable detail, these can illustrate a wide variety of harnesses, ranging from basic Flemish styles on the tombs of less affluent individuals through to magnificent images of fluted Gothic armour.

Much of the contemporary harness was imported from the Lowlands, although most of this originated in Milan or Nuremberg. Armouries in Italy boasted they could equip an 'Army' (albeit a fifteenth century army could number from just a few dozen to thousands) in a month and at regular arms fairs in Germany sufficient armour was on sale to equip thousands. The fact so much of this harness was interchangeable reinforces how artificial are some of the modern classifications as to type, particularly when mixed with older pieces. It is unclear how much

armour was manufactured in England; although armouries are recorded, their inventories either show a mix of imported, old and unprovenanced pieces of armour or they were specialists in making mail or linen armours (*Jacks*). Variations in national and regional styles are hinted at in the documentation, for example in the 1460s Household accounts of Sir John Howard and the Hoard accounts there is reference to Welsh and Scottish Jacks as well as normal Jacks. In the 1480s, Richard of Gloucester's northern soldiers were said to be dressed in old fashioned styles.

In attempting to classify the contemporary harness, the White Company's leading expert on armour, Mark Griffin, feels it might be more profitable to view it in terms of finish. White Harness required intense polishing to remove all hammer marks, it being common for water mills to be hired out for such tasks and to keep the harness bright. However, there was also 'Black' and 'Brown' or 'sanguine' harness. Whilst the difference between these two finishes was small,

In this picture an artist of the 'Gild of Saynte Luke' is painting a White Lion of March, another of Edward IV's badges, on a Pennon. In the foreground are the prepared pigments. The shape of the flag itself is in the form of a right-angled triangle. The style of identification, the sun at the hoist and the 'unit identification' (iiij) at the fly, was commonly used in the Burgundian Army. It is just supposition that it was used in England. Dave Key.

Here a skilled female member of the 'Gild of Saynte Luke' is putting the final touches to the White Lion of March's Pennon (Edward IV before he was king). Hanging over the front of the table is a completed Pennon painted in Edward IV's colours of blue and murrey with badges attributed to Edward on it. English Heritage.

Black Harness was essentially armour left black/rough from hammering, that is, not polished, although it would have been oiled and heated to ensure a carbonised finish to provide resistance to rust. Brown or Sanguine Harness was usually polished although its surface was then artificially rusted, 'sanguineing', that is the action of a chemical on the cold surface of the metal. This produced a cherry brown (references to red and brown were interchangeable in fifteenth century sources) coloured coat of carbon that was highly resistant to rust.

Alongside the debate over the classification of style is the question of whether the harness was lined. Given that they were designed to deflect direct blows to the head and thus required padding to absorb any transmission of kinetic energy, helmets always had either a quilted lining or were worn with a heavily padded and quilted arming cap. Where examples of this have survived they are invariably a garish red or pink, although no obvious reason for this is offered. Given all harness was worn over a padded arming doublet to provide support, an additional lining for the plate was less necessary. However, some examples have survived that have rivet holes around the edge that could possibly have been for attaching a lining. Care must be exercised as it was not unknown for such lining to be added in the seventeenth, eighteenth or even nineteenth century to provide a level of comfort unknown and out of place in the fifteenth. Equally, although some argue that a lining would reduce the noise of clanking metal, if harness makes such a noise it is a clear sign it has gaps and is not well made. Further, given the occasions for which harness was worn, it is difficult to understand why 'quiet' armour would offer much advantage!

Finally, one of the fundamental items that made fifteenth century battles so colourful were the numerous flags that were carried. The Banner, denoting the presence of a specific person, the Standard to identify a body of soldiers, and probably the most numerous style, the Pennon or 'Pensell'. These were small, typically triangular flags, and they seem to have been associated with small unit subdivisions. There is considerable evidence that within the army's division into three 'battles' the soldiers were organised into 'companies' of 100 men headed by a Captain, the unit being sub-divided into divisions of twenty men. The company could be denoted by a banner, standard or pennon (the terminology often varies) whilst each sub-division was identified by the smaller pennon. Thus in *View of Arms for the Leet of Conesford* for 27 June 1355 it is recorded that 'John Mountfort centenar, armed as above with lance and banner' whilst 'Thomas de Hornyngg, vintenar, armed with lance and pennon'. The *vintenar* had 18 men under his command and there were five *vintenar* in each *centenar*. Little had changed 100 years later as *The Coventry Leet Book*, in recording the city's troop preparations prior to the First Battle of St Albans, refers to about 100 men being led by a Captain (rather than a *centenar*) and there being issued a Pennon.

Most of the contemporary accounts, including Household accounts and documents relating to the Coronation of Richard III, indicate that pennons were cheap painted flags, although silk was also used, for example those for the Coventry soldiers. In contrast, the fewer Standards and Banners were far better made, those for Richard's coronation being made of *sarsynet* (plain silk) that was embroidered and gilded at a cost of 40s each. In contrast, the 750 Pennons made at the same time were constructed from *bokeram* (a cheap linen) and had badges added for a unit cost of just 4d, that is 1/120 the price of the standards. These same accounts indicate the Pennons were as small as twelve to eighteen inches in length as against the three yards

Here, a craftsman is painting the figure of Saint George slaying the dragon onto the linen that covered the limewood boards of a pavise. English Heritage.

of cloth provided for the standards. However, Continental references suggest two *ells* (54in if a Flemish *ell* is used) was more typical and most Pennons appear to have been around two to two and a half *ells* (54–68 inches if Flemish *ells*) long.

Corroborating evidence for these documentary sources comes from the various contemporary flags that of one sort or another have survived in collections. There is a surviving Standard of the City of Ghent in Belgium, although the most important collection was supplied by Charles the Bold, who was so comprehensively defeated by the Swiss that almost the entire set of Burgundian flags ended up in Swiss Museums. Comprehensive details of these were published in the 1960s in *Die Burgunderbutte*, which not only lists all equipment and paintings in Swiss museums but also drawings and photographs of items that have since fallen to pieces due to age.

Recently, the members of the *Company's* painters *Gild of Saynte Luke* (the patron saint of all painters due to the belief that he was the first to capture the image of Our Lady on canvas) expended considerable effort on reconstructing one of these small Pennons. As they were carried by groups of 10–20 soldiers, it is most appropriate for the numbers commonly fielded by the military element of the society. To maximise the occasion of reconstructing the Pennon, the *Company* organised a three-day living history event at King John's House in Romsey, Hampshire entitled 'Military Preparations for War'. Alongside men making mail, harness, Jacks and other military crafts, various persons busied themselves making the Pennon. Alongside the contemporary accounts and surviving items, the actual fifteenth century process of making a flag was recreated using the *Libro dell Arte* by Cennini, a contemporary handbook from Florence, on how to make, paint and gild a flag. Other sources were a manuscript in the Pepysian Library, a mid-fifteenth century manuscript from Strasbourg and an early sixteenth century East European painter's manual. Taking everything into consideration, an overall length of 54in was chosen and linen was used as the base. The linen was painted with original types of paints made from ground up pigment, only modern materials being resorted to if the original was too toxic. In keeping with the *Company's* generic Household identity, the Pennon was painted in Edward IV's colours of Blue and Murrey with badges attributed to Edward on it. *The Gild of Saynte Luke* is now completing a second, the Earl of March's Pennon (Edward IV before he was king). This displays the image of a lion, which has been carefully researched from tapestries, fonts and other pictorial sources to ensure it is a fifteenth century version of a lion and not the 'modern' Victorian image used by many re-enactors.

This approach of using living history techniques to produce equipment has enabled the society to make some of the finest replicas of medieval equipment, whether clothes made in a tailor's workshop or military *Pavises*. The *Pavises* are possibly the only accurate modern replicas of these 'shields' being made, comprising three wooden boards covered in linen and gesso and painted, or in one case painted and gilded with St George. The members of *The White Company* stress that the quality of their clothes and armour continues to benefit from the transfer of research and knowledge back and forth both with fellow groups, such as the *Companie of Saynte George*, *Wolfbane* and the *Lincoln Castle Longbowmen*, and with organisations like The Royal Armouries, Museum of London and the Wallace Collection, amongst many others.

English Civil War

With the decisive defeat of the Scots at Flodden in 1513, and apart from the serious Anglo-Scottish border clashes of the 1540s, there was no further significant fighting in mainland Britain until the Bishops Wars of 1639–40. Equally, with the conclusion of Henry VIII's various expeditions to France in the first half of the sixteenth century, England was to dispatch no further armies to the Continent for almost 80 years. Whilst thousands of English volunteers fought alongside the Dutch from the 1570s onwards, until the cataclysm of the Thirty Years' War, only the late Elizabethan conquest of Ireland offered significant military activity. However, although not directly involved in Continental warfare, due to the very significant numbers of English, Welsh, Scots and Irish mercenaries fighting for one or other side, the significant evolution in the military art was effectively communicated across the Channel. When Charles I initiated the First Bishop's War in 1639, all parts of the British Isles and Ireland were fully cognisant of contemporary military developments. Consequently, the various armies that marched back and forth across Britain and Ireland over the next eleven years of civil war were far from the amateur formations they are often made out to be. Often led and officered by professional soldiers, uniformed regiments, soon to be issued standardised equipment from military factories, waged a very modern war. Although regiments still bore the name of the colonel who had raised them and their standards often displayed an aspect of their heraldic coat of arms, their weapons, clothing and equipment were issued by the King or Parliament's centralised Ordinance Office. Military drills were soon standardised and as the war progressed more and more officers on both sides were appointed for their abilities rather than their social status. On the battlefield, the inability of armour to stop a musket ball saw the effective end of armour by the conclusion of the conflict for both pikemen and cavalrymen, as its weight was nothing but a pointless encumbrance.

In April 1645, England's first ever standing army was established, its regiments clothed in the familiar redcoats of the English soldier and its officers appointed by a central government to serve as full time professionals embarking on a career in the nation's service. This New Model Army, after defeating the Royalists and executing a brutal reconquest of Ireland, went on to lay the first tentative foundations of empire in the Caribbean. Although effectively disbanded with the fall of the Republic in 1660, Charles II immediately raised his small standing army from its remains, thereby establishing today's British Army.

Reflecting these crucial developments, the *Fairfax Battalia* (members of the *Roundhead Association* of the *English Civil War Society*) recreates all aspects of the clothes, equipment and arms of the professional soldier of the New Model Army. Composed of four separate regiments, Devereux's, Walton's, Foxe's and Overton's, the *Battalia* drills and fights as a single company of Sir Thomas Fairfax' Regiment of Foote, circa 1645. Regularly fielding at major musters around 150 men, their level of authenticity in clothes, equipment and drill is unsurpassed. The formation was created in the mid-1980s when members of Devereux's regiment came together with like-minded members of the other three regiments to form the *Fairfax Battalia* with the specific objective of creating a living history representation of the New Model Army of 1645–46. Achieving this without creating dissatisfaction amongst the individual members and ensuring that the four regiments did not lose their individual identity proved a very delicate business. What has been achieved today is a result of a group effort and a very fine balancing act. Take, for example, the re-equipping of the whole *Battalia* in a single style of red coat with a blue lining; while this was first suggested in 1990, it was not until 1993 that it was effected. Although the individual regiments still have

This full-length view of another *Fairfax* musketeer reveals the variations that would have existed even within the same company. Whilst his red coat and grey breeches are identical to his compatriot, he wears a knitted Monmouth cap whilst the bottles suspended from his bandoleer are unpainted. Equally, he has been issued a leather snapsack that is visible on his left side. Demonstrating that even the common soldiers' clothes reflected contemporary fashion, his breeches are open knee, the grey linen hose being tied up underneath with cord. Paul L. Isemonger.

Opposite.

This *Fairfax* musketeer is blowing on the ends of his match whilst awaiting the order to engage. He is clothed and equipped according to the various contracts recorded in the Ordinance Papers. The blue woollen lining of the Venice red coat is visible on the rolled back cuffs whilst the light blue painted bottles hang from his bandoleer on blue and white cord. The hilt of his sword, a simple Tuck, is visible on his left hip whilst a rolled blanket serves as a snapsack for his few personal possessions. The only item he is wearing that is not mentioned in the Ordinance Papers is his woollen Monteroe. Paul L. Isemonger.

This rear view of the same musketeer reveals the various items of equipment that hung from the shoulders. His straight bladed Tuck would be described as of 'Munition' quality, that is a mass-produced item for the common soldier. Resting on the canvas bag is a small leather water bottle, whilst the canvas bag itself would contain various items of spare clothing and food. Just visible beneath the linen bag is the leather snapsack containing more of the same. Paul L. Isemonger.

their own distinctive coats for their own separate events, these are seldom now worn.

In respect of the *Battalia's* drill, with the expert guidance of John Litchfield, it follows the contemporary English derivative of the Dutch model to the letter and strives to reproduce the contemporary method of fighting, only compromising in fundamental areas of safety. It is here that the *Battalia* becomes obviously distinctive to the casual observer from other English Civil War groups. The detail of the contemporary drill is used even where not strictly necessary for the purpose of battle re-enactments. Ensuring that each file is drawn-up with the correct use of 'dignity' and that all the evolutions are used is reflective of a desire to display to the audience how a contemporary unit would have operated. Fighting at point of pike is authentic

With their captain in the lead, the *Fairfax Battalia* re-create a company of Sir Thomas Fairfax's Regiment as they advance upon the enemy with the pike to the rear ready to protect the musket if advanced upon by cavalry. Although there is a degree of uniformity in respect of coats and breeches, and the entire block of musket have bandoleers, the latter have various finishes, some painted, some plain. Equally there is some variation in headgear, with a mix of Monmouth caps and broad-brim felt hats. To the right of the officer is the sergeant of musket keeping an eye on the ranks, armed with the badge of his rank, a halbert. English Heritage.

although it does restrict the competitiveness beloved of those re-enactors who use the comport push of pike (pikes held up across the body). Their flanking wings of shot maintain their correct position alongside the pike even if this restricts the flow of the battle with opponents awkwardly placed too close. In this, the *Battalia* is fortunate in having a counterpart in the guise of the *Marquis of Winchester's Regiment of Foot*, members of *the King's Army* in the *English Civil War Society*. Sharing the *Battalia's* ethos, *Winchester's* enables the *Battalia* to engage in the manner that they wish, whilst the remainder of the *English Civil War Society* carry on in the more familiar competitive manner. Essentially, the emphasis for the *Battalia* and

Winchester's is that they are a living history representation that also participates in battle re-enactment.

It would be fair to say that by the 1630s the clothes of a typical contemporary soldier was fairly standard throughout the British Isles. Despite popular perception, English, Scots and Irish soldiers were clothed in similar styles, albeit with a number of minor regional variations. However, for those seeking to reconstruct the ordinary soldier of the English Civil War there has long been the major problem that no known soldier's clothes have survived to this age. It is ironic that there are more surviving items for a first century Roman legionary or a Dark Ages Romano-British warrior than for the soldier who fought at Naseby just 350 years ago. Whilst durable items such as weapons, buff coats, metal helmets and the odd piece of equipment such as bandoleers and belts have survived, only a handful of clothes belonging to wealthy civilians grace national collections. The only handful of clothes for lower orders comes from a few bog finds in Scotland and Ireland. There is not even much in the way of pictorial evidence for the ordinary soldier, the portraiture of the age concerning itself solely with the wealthy sitter. However, thanks to the pioneering research of Alan Turton and Stuart

Having completed the day's march a soldier would divest himself of his equipment. Laid out here on the leather snapsack and linen bag are the personal items of a typical musketeer, including a spare pair of shoes, his knife, wooden plate and eating utensils, and other miscellaneous items. Paul L. Isemonger.

Peachey it is now possible to offer a well-provenanced reconstruction of an English Civil War soldier.

Equally, in reconstructing the specific clothes and equipment of a soldier of the New Model Army, the *Battalia* is fortunate in having almost the complete set of contracts to survive from its inception in April 1645 to almost the end of the war in March 1646. The volumes containing the contracts were almost lost in the early 1800s when the Ordnance Office in the Tower threw out these notebooks as 'waste paper'. Fortunately they were saved by a Benjamin Nicholson and are today available in the British Library. These documents reveal that in clothing, equipping and arming the New Model Army, the novel idea of standardisation was introduced and this is reflected in the clothes and equipment of the *Battalia*. It was required that manufacturers had to provide set patterns of their products which they were held to match in mass production and to deliver to the Tower

of London for inspection. Consequently many of the contracts specified remarkable detail for whatever the item may have been and also demonstrated how London had developed what can only be described as a varied and substantial military industry capable of rapidly delivering both quantity and quality. From mid 1645 through to 1646 the totals delivered were remarkable, 8,050 matchlock muskets, 3,300 firelock muskets, 5,600 pikes, 10,200 coats/cassacks, 9,000 shirts, 20,200 snapsacks and 23,700 pairs of shoes.

Commencing at the top, there were essentially three types of common headwear, the Monmouth cap, the monteroe and the broad-brimmed felt, or beaver hat, metal helmets being reserved for battle. The former was undoubtedly the most common, 26,000 Monmouth caps being sent in 1641 and 1642 to the English troops in Ireland, manufactured at 23/-a dozen. Whilst there was no specific record of any being distributed before Edgehill, after Brentford a quantity of these hats were definitely issued from the Irish stores in London to Essex's men. Knitted from about 1lb of wool, then felted, Symonds wrote of their manufacture at Bewdley in 1644:

'The only manufacture of this town is making of caps called Monmouth caps, knitted by poor people for twopence apiece, ordinary ones sold for two

By the time the New Model Army was first being equipped in April–May 1645 the use of armour by the pike was in decline. Although some continued to wear the armour previously issued, no new issue was recorded in the Ordinance Papers. Here, some of *Fairfax's* pike practice advancing at point and whilst all wear helmets, only a small proportion wear back and breast plates. Having said this, one of the leading pikeman still retains the tassets to his back and breast to protect his upper legs, an unusual sight by 1645. English Heritage.

shillings, three shillings, and four shillings. First they are knit, then they mill them, then block them, then they work with tassels, then they sheer them'. When complete they had a moderately broad brim and probably had a leather hatband inside this to prevent the wool irritating the forehead. These warm and practical hats were undoubtedly popular with soldiers of both sides, with a common brimless variation to allow them to be worn under metal helmets.

Monteroes were equally popular, particularly with the Royalists, although there was no single variant of it. This hat probably originated in France earlier in the century and they generally resembled a jockey hat with two brims fore and aft. Some variants operated almost like a balaclava with a brim that could be pulled down around the face and back of the head. The

ordinary soldiers' versions were manufactured from wool cloth whilst officers' versions were commonly made from velvet and decorated with lace. The third type of headgear was the broad-brim felt hat. There are no records of these having been issued to common soldiers, although the gentry and officers certainly commonly wore them. The superior versions were meant to be manufactured from beaver skin imported from North America, and even when not, were constructed from high quality felt. If heavily fulled and felted, the Monmouth hat provided a cheap imitation.

Next came the core of any soldier's clothing–the coat. While many soldiers began fighting in their

Opposite.

These pikeman could not be better equipped. They have the full set of armour including well-proportioned tassets. Both have straight-bladed Tucks and one even has a small hand axe for cutting wood. Nonetheless, despite sharing the issue coats with the musket, variations are obvious in terms of clothes, one wearing grey cloth cut woollen hose, the other woollen knitted hose. Whilst apparently ready for combat, it is to be doubted if they would have carried all their personal equipment into action. The blanket rolls and linen bags would most likely have been left with the regimental baggage. Paul L. Isemonger.

Here a group of *Fairfax's* musket and pike reflect the variation within a single company—other than the issue coats, no two are identical. The rear view of the pikeman shows the browned helmet suspended from the back plate of his armour as well as his bulging snapsack. Although grey breeches were issued with the coats these appear to have soon worn out and it would appear the pikeman has acquired a civilian pair. The black leather water bottle at the rear of one of the musketeers is another example of a civilian item common to soldiers of the time. Paul L. Isemonger.

civilian clothes, military clothes were issued to most at some point. These were commonly issued as suits and could include breeches, shirts, stockings and monteroes. Both coats and breeches were commonly made from dense wool broadcloth, the former lined either with a lighter weight wool or linen, the latter only with linen. Other materials used for coats were Kersey, a wool cloth described as 'a base and course kind of cloth for the use of poor people', and canvas. While there was no precise pattern for soldiers' coats, they closely reflected the straight cut style of the common labourers' coats, albeit with a number of more specifically military features. There appear to have been two broad variations, one with the outside

Opposite.

This individual pikeman of *Fairfax's* appears as he would have been for the march. He has taken off his helmet that is suspended from a hook on the rear of his armour and wears instead just a knitted woollen cap. It should be noted that, despite appearances, his helmet is not rusty, rather it has been purposely 'browned' in a chemical solution to prevent rusting. A canvas snapsack bulges with extra clothes, food and personal items on his back whilst his knitted woollen hose have been pulled up over the ends of his breeches to keep out the draughts. Paul L. Isemonger.

made of two yards of Kersey, the other of one and one-third yards of Broadcloth. The key variation lay in the linings and fastening systems.

Thanks to the research of Stuart Peachey and Alan Turton details for these come from two particularly detailed accounts for 7,400 suits provided by England for the Scots Army in September 1644. Taking the totals of materials used to complete the order divided by the number produced, each suit used approximately two yards of broadcloth or an equivalent area of kersey, two yards of linen or lockram lining, a pair of leather pockets, 36 buttons and six pairs of hooks. A slightly less detailed return originated from Commissary George Wood in December 1645 for two options for 'magazine' suits (Wood can be seen as an

experienced operator having been involved in earlier shipping clothes to Ireland). For the first option he listed for each suit, 3H yards of northern kersey, 1H yards of lindsay cloth for lining the breeches and a pair of leather pockets. He set aside 1Hd for the tape binding the coat and for knee strings, and 1d for buttons and hooks for breeches (a penny's worth of hooks, eyes and buttons could purchase 6 hooks and eyes and 6 buttons). For the second option he listed 4 yards of northern kersey or $2^{11}/_{32}$nd yards of broadcloth, 1H yards of lockram and a pair of leather pockets. He set aside 2d for the tape binding the coat, 2d for the knee strings and 1d for the hooks and buttons for the breeches.

Opposite.

Responsible for drill and keeping the common soldier in order, this sergeant of pike carries a halbert, the badge of his rank. Otherwise he is clothed and equipped in identical fashion to the remainder of the ranks. Although sashes and privately purchased clothes are mentioned for sergeants in some accounts, these relate to sergeants of the trained bands, often affluent skilled artisans and the like. As the war progressed, in the regular field regiments sergeants were promoted from the ranks for their ability and consequently wore what they were issued. Paul L. Isemonger.

A significant part of the English Civil War involved sieges rather than battles and in the closing stages of the conflict, much of the New Model Army's efforts were directed to mopping up the surviving Royalist strongholds. Here, musketeers from *Fairfax* are assisting on the siege lines. Often involved in sniping at enemy sentries, the musketeer in the foreground is using a musket rest to steady his aim, almost the only occasion in the late war that a rest would still have been used. To the right of the picture, a sapper in heavy siege armour is exposed to enemy fire as he shovels soil into the wicker gabion and it is likely the musketeers are attempting to provide some degree of suppressing fire on the sapper's behalf. English Heritage.

Between the Scots' coats and those of Wood there are several noticeable differences in terms of materials. Firstly, the number of buttons were reduced from 36 to about six and these were all specifically for the breeches. These buttons could have been small white metal items or simply twisted pieces of cloth around a tiny piece of bone or the like. Secondly, there was sufficient lining material for the breeches but not the coat. Finally, while hooks were provided for the breeches, there do not appear to have been any eyes. Thus the Scots coats probably had 30 closely spaced small buttons down the front of the coat with the

Once the battery position gabionage for the siege guns was finished, Sakers and other heavy guns were moved into position to demolish sections of wall. Whilst the musketeers continue to snipe at the enemy, in the background a Saker has been positioned in preparation for the bombardment, its crew protected by soil-filled wicker gabions. English Heritage.

remaining 6 closing the fly on the breeches. In terms of pattern there was less variation, with apparently most coats made to a single size from one yard of cloth with a width of sixty inches. Coats were cut straight without a waist to reach down to just below the hip to minimise waste and complexity thus permitting rapid mass production by semi-skilled labour. Sleeves were long enough to be rolled back to reveal the lining, often with a small slit at the wrist to facilitate this. There was a short collar around one-inch high and shoulder rolls or 'wings' where the sleeve entered the body of the coat. The latter appears to have been a specifically military feature. Finally there were normally two internal pockets in the lining, often made from leather.

In some references, 'cassacks' rather than coats were specified and it appears the terms were interchangeable. Technically the term cassack referred to a Dutch style of garment that could be converted from a coat to a cloak with buttons both down the sleeves and under the arms. Such garments were noticeably more voluminous and thus more expensive than a simple coat, requiring three or more yards of broadcloth for the outer layer and five to six yards for the lining. In addition, they required a considerable number of buttons, anything up to 180 if the sleeves, front, sides and rear were to be operated. Whilst such Dutch style cassacks were undoubtedly worn by officers, only specialist units such as the Earl of Essex's guard were issued with such.

The shorter doublets were also a common civilian item of wear many soldiers brought with them upon enrolment and a number were manufactured and issued as military coats. Made from wool or linen canvas and lined in linen, they commonly had six to eight hanging tabs. Although they cost around a quarter less than a coat, 6s as opposed to between 8–11s, their shorter length and narrower cut appears to have made them less favoured amongst the rank and file. Many portraits of officers show them wearing fashionable versions.

Whether part of a suit of clothes or issued separately, breeches were invariably made of broadcloth or kersey and lined with white or brown linen. Given the need to reduce costs, the common

Large and small guns alike would bombard the walls for days or weeks before a practicable breach was achieved. With little to do at this stage, a pikeman from *Fairfax* watches the gunners at work from behind the safety of the gabions. Whilst he has left his snapsack and other items behind in camp, he wears his armour to give himself an added feeling of security, despite the fact it would have been incapable of stopping a musket ball. Only the far heavier siege armour, often three to four times the weight of ordinary armour, could offer any degree of safety from musket balls. English Heritage.

soldier's versions were not particularly baggy, but rather loose fitting and generally cut to a universal length of around 31Hin. They normally had tapestrings to tie them closed at the knee and a pair of leather pockets similar to those in the coat. The fly was normally closed by 6 buttons and around 6 pairs of hooks and/or eyes were sewn to the waistband to attach the breeches to the coat or doublet.

In respect of what colour coats and breeches were expected to be dyed, it appears red was already well established as the military colour for English troops. While Cecil C.P. Lawson in the first volume of his *Uniforms of the British Army* demonstrated that there was some evidence for a preference for red coats and breeches during the latter part of the Elizabethan era,

blue was equally popular. Certainly in the fighting against the Spanish in the Low Countries, the English soldiers under John Morris, Sir Philip Sidney, Lord Willoughby and Sir Francis Vere wore red cassacks. In 1585 the City of London equipped troops for service in the Low Countries in red coats and in 1590 troops in Canterbury had their yellow coats changed to red. By the eve of the First Bishop's War in 1638, red appears to have become the accepted colour for soldiers coats as it was requested that, 'It would be good if Yr.Lordship's men had red breeches to their buff coats, because otherwise being country fellows they will not be so neartly habited as the other Lord's men'. Later, as the Civil War itself erupted, although possibly referring to the coats of his own regiment, Denzill Holles' Sergeant Nehemiah Wharton on 13 September 1642 referred to, 'The countryman I clothed in a soldier's red coate'.

Red continued to be favoured when available, being effectively institutionalised with the coming of the New Model in 1645/46.The Ordnance papers even provide some detail for the construction of the New Model Army's legendary uniform red coats. An example was that of 14 February 1645/46 with Richard Downs of London: 'Two Thousand Coates and Two Thousand Breeches at seventeen shillings a

Above and opposite.

Away from the siege lines the many women who helped keep the soldiers in the field have managed to establish a somewhat more substantial camp than they might otherwise on the march. Here food is being prepared under a canvas-shelter a necessary protection from the cold and wet weather of the seventeenth century's mini iceage. Such scenes of domesticity were common given the long periods most soldiers spent in camp. English Heritage.

Coat & Breeches. Two Thousand paire of stockins at Thirteene pence halfe penny a paire. The coates to be of a Red Colour and of Suffolke, Coventry or Gloucester-shire Cloth and to be made Three quarters & a nayle long (29Gin) faced with bayse or Cotton with tapestrings according to a pattern delivered into ye said Committee.

The Breeches to be of Grey or some other good Coloure & made of Reading Cloth or other Cloth in length Three quarters one eight well lined and Trimmed sutable to ye patternes presented, the said Cloth both of ye Coates and of ye Breeches to be first shrunke in Cold water.'

Further support for the predominance of red comes from the recorded importation into Bristol between 1613 and 1655 of around 17,500lb of madder from Amsterdam per annum. As a single pound of madder could dye up to 10lb of wool red and an average soldier's coat weighed approximately 3lb, there was sufficient madder coming just into Bristol to dye 58,000 coats per year. Even deducting the use of some of this madder for civilian clothes, there was ample for military needs.

For the *Battalia*, this plethora of sources has required some synthesis of the evidence to produce both an accurate yet affordable set of military clothes. Taking the clothes detailed in the Ordnance Papers and the general shape illustrated in a woodcut of an English soldier in Ireland, John Litchfield has produced the necessary pattern. The resulting red woollen coat is 29Hin long and cut straight, with 10 pewter buttons, shoulder rolls and rolled back cuffs displaying the blue wool lining. Breeches are mostly grey or brown, although reflecting the fact that some Royalist soldiers deserted to the New Model Army, a few wear the red breeches that Royalist soldiers received as part of their red suit of clothes. Whilst to save money the basic seams of the coat and breeches are machine stitched, the buttonholes and visible stitching is hand finished. However, an increasing number of members are now taking the basic cut out panels and hand stitching the entire coat and breeches.

While a common item of wear for officers, waistcoats were occasionally issued to common soldiers. These were manufactured from almost anything that came to hand, wool cloth, linen and even old canvas or leather wall hangings. Generally these were very simply cut, being short and without sleeves, although they did occasionally have four hanging tabs in the style of the doublet with a short collar. The *Battalia's* soldiers are encouraged to wear these and other items of civilian clothing under their military clothes in order to reflect that these 'soldiers' had only recently been civilians and that the distinction in the mid-seventeenth century between soldier and civilian was grey at best.

As for the small clothes, the shirts were commonly made from lockram or Osnaburg linen (linen could be made from hemp or flax) and cut generally from ten foot lengths between 36 and 42in wide to essentially a single fit all size. With gussets added at the end of the neck, chest and thigh splits to resist tearing, and the cuffs were simply gathered at the wrist with a small collar added to prevent the neck being chaffed by the woollen coat.

Stockings or hose were made from either cotton or wool, the former being cut out, the latter being knitted or made from loosely woven woollen cloth.

Generally white or grey in colour, woollen stockings/hose could weigh as much as 9oz per pair. At present the *Battalia* is re-equipping in woollen cloth cut hose as the sources indicate these were the most common issue to soldiers. However, these are mixed with woollen hand knitted hose made to an original seventeenth century pattern to reflect the diversity of clothes worn by contemporary soldiers.

As for the soldiers' primary weapon, although manufactured by hand, there were recognised specifications for the standard musket. In 1639, the gunsmiths of London, in confirming orders for 15,000 new matchlocks for the Bishop's War describe '5,000 to be of the larger size, or four feet in the barrel…and 10,000 of the shorter, or 3H feet'. These standardised dimensions are confirmed by surviving muskets in the Tower, which conform to these specified lengths of barrel (by 1645 the forked musket rest had fallen out of use as muskets became lighter). Reproductions of these 'Tower' matchlocks are available from a variety of gunsmiths for between £200–£300. As for the pike, given the *Battalia* mostly fights at point in scripted displays, properly turned steel tipped pikes are carried by the pikemen. To date there has been no injury as a result, the very fact of the steel tip causing soldiers to take added care. When the *Battalia* does participate in

If the garrison did not capitulate, the culmination of a siege was the storm. Having divested themselves of snapsack and other baggage, these musketeers deliver fire as the pike storm the breach. They would have then butted their muskets and drawn swords before adding their presence to the pikemen in the breach. English Heritage.

battle re-enactments, the hobby's safe' wooden or rubber tipped pikes are carried. Finally, all soldiers carry 'munition' quality swords, either a straight bladed 'tuck' or curved bladed 'hanger' that can be purchased for approximately £100 from a variety of suppliers.

Possibly the single most important item for any soldier alongside his weapon was his shoes. For the infantry there were broadly two types, shoes proper and 'startups'. While many portraits of the wealthy illustrate a square-toed shoe with cutaway sides, this undoubtedly reflected a fashionable model. For the common soldier their shoes were round toed with closed sides made for strength rather than fashion, with a low heel. Made from the hides of bovine animals such as cows and ox, they were manufactured as straights, that is there was no right or left shoes in a pair, all were identical in shape. Mass produced in their thousands, particularly in Northampton and

London, shoes had a life expectancy of at most three months during the campaign season. Soldiers of all armies would count themselves lucky if they received more than two pairs in any given year. As for startups, these were essentially calf-length boots that laced or buttoned up the front and were the common wear of rural agricultural workers. Whilst there are no records of startups being manufactured or issued to soldiers, it is certain many, particularly those forced to rely on their civilian clothes in default of military issue, wore these comfortable and practical items. Consequently, whilst most soldiers in the *Battalia* wear the straight lasted military shoe, some do wear startups to reflect the fact these men were often obliged to continue wearing their own civilian clothes. Given the cost for the new recruit, the *Battalia* maintains a slop-chest of hand stitched shoes made by Sarah Juniper so that from day one they have the appropriate footwear.

Whilst not strictly speaking an item of clothing, most soldiers appear to have been supplied with a snapsack when issued clothing and shoes. Whilst variations in pattern existed, those issued to the military generally resembled a duffel bag style tube or 'sausage', which was slung by a strap over the shoulder. These were normally made of leather or canvas and were substantial in proportions.

Commonly, alongside personal items and food, a diligent soldier would carry a spare shirt, pair of shoes, stockings and other items of spare clothing in their snapsack. Soldiers of Essex's army in September 1643 each carried 3 days worth of provisions in theirs when marching to the relief of Gloucester, a weight in itself of between 4–9lb.

The Ordnance papers for the new Model Army prove that all musketeers were supplied with bandoleers, over 24,000 being contracted. One example details that; 'The Boxes of the said 2000 Bandileers to bee of wood wth whole Bottoms to bee turned wthin and not bored, the Heade to bee of wood and to bee layd in oyle, vizt Three times over and to bee coloured blew wth blew and white strings, wth strong thred twist and wth good belts att XXd a peece to bee brought into the Tower of London, and to bee received imediately...'. Not all the bandoleers though were manufactured from wood as 4,000 were of either iron or copper plate and unusually all were from one supplier, suggesting specialist skills, as on 7 January 1645/46: 'There contracted wth Thomas Jupe, Thomas Roch & Nathaniell Humfreys of Michaells Crooked Lane for 4,000 Bandeleers the boxes of strong double plate the heads the same wth whipcord string & with good Belts according to the patterne at 20d apeece to be brought into the Tower of London...'. To reflect this contemporary variety of bandoleers, although around half in the *Battalia* are the blue turned bottles referred to above, the remainder are a mix of types.

The Ordnance Papers also detail for the *Battalia* what might be termed the miscellaneous items of drums, colours, halberts and partisans, which were ordered from specialising suppliers of such. The following order, amongst the Ordnance papers of the New Model, was dated 16 December 1644 and referred to Colonel Edward Aldriche's new colours which were produced as a result of the Parliamentary defeat at Lostwithiel. When Essex's Army was integrated into the New Model, Aldriche took his new colours with him: 'There is due unt Alexander Vener Ensigne Maker ye summe of Eighteene pounds To be pd out of such moneys as Remayne in ye hands of Sr Walter Erle Knt Lieutenent gen. of ye Ordnce Recd by him at Habberdashers hall for ye buying of Drums, Ensignes, partizans & Halberts for ye Lord Generalls Army (By Order from ye Comons House of Parlyamt dat 28 Nov 1644) ffor ye buying Drums, Cullers, Halberts & partizans for ye furnishing of Collonell Aldrich his Regimt. vizt ffor VII new Ensignes made of blew florence sarsnett wth Distinctions of gold culler Laurells wth tassells to yem.'

Sheltering from enemy snipers behind the log shield, this *Fairfax* musketeer awaits a target of opportunity. The smouldering match cord is looped through the fingers of his left hand whilst the palm of his right protects the powder in the pan. It will take him but a moment to fix the match in the jaws of the serpent and fire. English Heritage.

Although the *Battalia* carries just a single company colour of Sir Thomas Fairfax's Regiment, there is some controversy over whether his regimental colours were green or blue, so the *Battalia* have a version of each. However, reflecting the course of this ongoing debate, in recent years the 'blew florence sarsnett' (plain silk) colour is commonly flown.

Thus the *Battalia* is able to reflect how, the soldiers of Parliament's New Model Army were finally able to take the surrender of the few remaining Royalist garrisons, fully equipped to the most modern of standards. Its infantry were universally clothed in red coats, grey breeches and well shod, each regiment with its distinctive coat lining colour displayed at the cuff. Whilst its shot and pike were fully armed to the established 2:1 ratio, there was apparently no armour, be it back and breasts or helmets, worn by the latter.

Napoleonic Wars

Be they the British redcoats of Wellington's Army or the blue coated infantry of Napoleon's Imperial forces, there is little doubt that the Napoleonic Wars still evoke tremendous interest. In many respects this conflict was the culmination of the gunpowder age.

The 68th company officer standing behind his men wears a scarlet, green faced jacket made from high quality superfine woollen cloth. His jacket is further distinguished with over 12yds of silver metallic lace, wings and silver ball buttons stamped with the regimental design. When the crimson silk sash, regimental sword and other specific items are added, such quality reproductions involve no small expense. English Heritage.

The decades of debate and experimentation between linear tactics with its emphasis on the deployment of firepower, literally went head to head with those who promoted the speed and impact of the column. Originating with Dutch tactical deployment in the mid-seventeenth century, the British and Prussian Armies in particular had, by the late eighteenth century, evolved a sophisticated firing system that maximised the weight of fire a body of troops could bring to bear on an enemy. Whilst the French Army had not rejected this type of deployment (indeed the various national drill manuals of the period are almost identical in their essential small arms, company and battalion evolutions), they had come to favour the

Awaiting their officer's orders, these soldiers of the re-created *68th Durham Light Infantry* are the archetypal image of the eponymous thin red line. Although the 68th were a specialist light infantry regiment, they were still trained to fight in close order alongside standard line infantry. However, as a light infantry regiment they retained the stovepipe shako in 1812 when line infantry regiments adopted the distinctive Belgic shako. English Heritage.

battlefield tactic of the column.

This conflict also witnessed the refinement of dispersed light infantry tactics that had equally been evolving throughout the latter half of the eighteenth century. Commencing with the irregular formations of the Austrian, Russian and Prussian armies of the Seven Years' War, and particularly focused for both the British and French armies in their conflicts in North America, by 1789 all European armies had established bodies of light troops. Experience in Flanders 1793–95 and subsequently in the Caribbean for the British Army and in conflicts ranging across the breadth of Europe for the French saw the refinement of both their light infantry. By the time their soldiers met in the Peninsular no column or line was complete without its screen of skirmishers.

Alongside developments in the technical quality and tactical use of artillery, the shape of warfare was then set for the next half century. Military officers in Europe and America were educated using the tactical and strategic lessons of the Napoleonic Wars as related in the works of Clausewitz and Jomini. Such was the legacy that the American armies of North and South that fought what many have called the first modern war between 1861–65 were in fact led by officers entrenched in the tactical doctrines of Napoleon. Their soldiers learnt an arms drill that was little more than a modified form of that taught to the soldiers of Wellington and Napoleon, and on the battlefield the mass volleys of muskets were still how most soldiers delivered their fire whilst deployed shoulder to shoulder in line. Only with the introduction of the breach-loaded rifle as the predominate infantry weapon from the mid 1860s alongside breech-loaded artillery firing explosive shells did the Napoleonic age finally fade.

The story of the redcoat stretches from the mid-seventeenth century through to the men who maintained Queen Victoria's vast global empire. However, there is little doubt that the British redcoats' greatest era was that of the Napoleonic Wars when the 'thin red line' confronted the apparently unstoppable columns of the French Army. Specifically

Here a young soldier of the 68th is priming the pan of his Brown Bess musket from a cartridge he has just removed from his leather cartridge box on his left hip. The blue painted canteen has both the regimental and company designation in white whilst details of the waxed canvas backpack can also be seen. As packs were normally dropped when action was to be joined this is likely just a drill session. English Heritage.

This immaculately turned out grizzled veteran of the 68th would have been a valued member of any company. The square-ended regimental lace with its specific regimental coloured stripes can clearly be seen on his chest as can the pewter buttons stamped with the numeral '68' and the square brass belt plate. The other distinguishing features of a light infantry regiment are the stamped brass bugle horn on the front of the shako with green plume and the wings on each shoulder of the jacket. English Heritage.

commemorating two of northern England's most famous regiments are the *68th Durham Light Infantry Display Team* and the *33rd Foot, The Duke of Wellington's (West Riding Regiment)*. The former originated in 1975 when a handful of members of the DLI Regimental Association decided to form a 68th Society to keep alive the history and traditions of the old DLI after its absorption in 1968 into the Light Infantry Regiment. From this society was born the *68th DLI Display Team*, which has since taken on the active roll of demonstrating at living history events both the light infantry drill of the latter part of the Napoleonic Wars and the everyday life of Wellington's soldiers.

Rightly renowned for the quality of their clothes and equipment, there is as great an emphasis in the *68th* on the detail of the contemporary arms and company drill so vital on the battlefield. The thirty or

so members meet regularly to collectively practice both light and line drill movements. All these movements are taken from the manuals in the possession of the team. These include for the line: *Rules and Regulations for the formations, field exercise and movements,* 1798 (Dundas); *Manual and Platoon exercise,* 1804 and 1812 editions; *Rules and Regulations for the Manual and Platoon exercises, formations, field exercise and movements,* 1807 and 1811 editions. For the Light Infantry: *Light Infantry Exercise 1797; Regulations for the exercise of Riflemen and Light Infantry,* 1803 and 1808 editions; *A course of Drill and Instruction in the Duties of Light Infantry,* 1808 edition; *Instructions for Light Infantry and Riflemen,* by Neil Campbell 1813; and *finally Drill and Manoeuvres as practised by the 52nd Light Infantry,* by John Cross.

Having loaded, the soldiers await the officer's order to fire. Further details of the officer's jacket are visible including the distinctive light infantry wings. Equally, being an officer of light infantry, the tails of his jacket are cut short and he carries a sabre with the 68th's regimental badge emblazoned on its silver hilt. The nearest soldier is the company pioneer, distinguished by his brown leather apron and the Billhook worn on a waistbelt. English Heritage.

Indeed, the *68th* has in its possession a fine collection of drill manuals for the period besides works by Barber and Cooper, in addition to copies of unpublished manuals, notebooks and diaries. This collection provides an excellent view of the evolution of the Light Infantry drill and how the excesses of the eighteenth century drill evolved to the hard practicalities of the early nineteenth century.

Apart from the *68th*, which was a light infantry regiment, one small criticism levelled by some Napoleonic re-enactors of many recreated British regiments is that they tend to reconstruct elite companies, be they grenadiers or light infantry. During the actual wars such troops in fact represented only around 10 per cent of Wellington's infantry, the vast bulk being the ordinary centre companies. An exception to the general trend is the *33rd Foot*, in that

they do focus upon a centre company. The *33rd* was formed in 1995 around a core of experienced re-enactors and today has around 25 members including as its chairman, John Spencer, the curator of the Duke of Wellington's Regimental Museum. One of the *33rd's* key members is Keith Raynor, possibly one of Britain's leading researchers on British infantry of the Napoleonic era. Given that Keith was the principal researcher of the *68th* and that a number of other *33rd* members were long serving participants in the *68th*, the two societies work closely together, offering between them what is undoubtedly the two finest reconstructions of Wellington's Redcoats.

Although able to offer a range of impressions, from the early 1800s through to Waterloo, the *33rd* concentrates its efforts on representing the ordinary centre company soldier as he appeared in 1815 just after the regiment's return from India. Originally formed in 1702 at the start of the Spanish War of Succession, the 33rd was stationed in India from 1796 to 1811. In 1806, Sir Arthur Wellesley, the future Duke of Wellington, was promoted to Colonel on the death of the previous incumbent, the Marquis Cornwallis (this illustrious connection is celebrated in the regiment's modern title, 'The Duke of Wellington's'). The 33rd's return to England from

The classic image of Wellington's redcoats is the square and here Vistula Lancers have forced a detached company of the 68th to form back to back for safety. With just a handful of enemy cavalry, these men are fairly safe, although as they are Lancers, they can thrust over the hedge of bayonets until they are shot from their saddles. English Heritage.

India coincided with the general standardisation that took place regarding the army's accoutrements and uniforms between 1811 and 1813, the 33rd being clothed and equipped according to the new regulations before being dispatched to Stralsund in 1813 under General Thomas Graham. The 33rd saw much hard fighting under Graham in the 1814 campaign in Holland, the regiment remaining in the Low Countries into 1815 hence being fully involved in the final Waterloo campaign. As part of General Sir Colin Halkett's Brigade, the 33rd suffered heavy losses at both Quatre Bras and Waterloo.

One of the major advantages in reconstructing the uniform of the 33rd for the latter part of the Napoleonic Wars, is that the regiment was re-equipped over a short period of time. This contrasts with the regiments serving in the Peninsular, who received their new issues of clothing and equipment intermittently. However, this has not meant that a simple reproduction of the 1812–15 British infantry uniform is sufficient if a correct impression is to be achieved. The reality was that despite all items of uniform and accoutrements having to be made to a sealed pattern, many articles of clothing and equipment were still produced by hand allowing for slight variations. Also, conditions in the 'field' might mean *ad hoc* appearances, such as when Greatcoats have to be made out of blankets. There was also the fact that regimental pride and the influence of some colonels on *their* regiment, ensured that a few units were more 'distinguished' than others. In both co-ordinating and undertaking much of the primary research, Keith Raynor has had to call upon a broad pool of researchers involved in the period who over the years have come to trust each other in sharing the fruits of their research.

To find the details needed to reconstruct the appearance of the Regiment's uniform, Keith Raynor commenced with the various War Office documents in the Public Record Office at Kew, relating to both the 33rd and Army Regulations. Equally, the *Journal of the Society for Army Historical Research* is a good source for pointers and has printed some excellent articles and notes over the years concerning uniforms of this period. Interestingly, the archives stored at the

National Army Museum in Chelsea are not that useful for this period, though the United Services Museum in Edinburgh is helpful, particularly as its small number of staff appear always under pressure. Outside Britain, the Canadian Archives are excellent and again the staff is helpful. Keith is fortunate in being able to visit Canada at least twice a year and his circle of friends is invaluable in pursuing various items of information. Back in England, the Duke of Wellington's Regimental Museum in Halifax has many documents relating to the Regiment at this period with some also pertaining to the 76th Foot, later the 'Dukes' Second Battalion. Keith finds it ironic that there is far more specifically on the 76th, particularly as that unit had in some ways a more varied and interesting Napoleonic career, first serving with the

Holding their India pattern Brown Bess muskets at the Shoulder Arms, this front view of these soldiers of the 33rd shows the regiment's distinctive single spaced bastion ended loops and red facings. Although the style of stamped brass GR plate on the Belgic shako was universal, that of the 33rd was distinguished by the numerals '33' below the sovereign's initials. The other distinctive item is the stamped oval brass plates worn on the front of the bayonet belt that bore the regimental numerals within a crowned garter belt.

K MacFarlane.

33rd in India. It then returned to Europe in 1807, serving first in the Walcheren Expedition in 1809 and then to the Peninsular in 1813. It concluded its wartime service in Canada, fighting at Plattsburg in 1814.

With respect to original pieces, there are only a few surviving articles relating to the 33rd. There is an original officer's cross-belt plate, a button for the period 1812–15, a sergeant's sash worn at Waterloo, and an other rank's Belgic shako plate. The latter proves that the basic 1812 Regulation pattern was adhered too, though the large Arabic numerals '33' below the GR on the plate, have meant that the GR is smaller in comparison to that on the Army's sealed pattern plate. Also, there is a French Army clothes brush picked up from the field of Waterloo by one of the 33rd! There are numerous surviving coats and other artefacts from various regiments spread throughout collections in Britain and overseas, and in conjunction with contemporary tailoring books, highly accurate reconstructions are possible.

Given the paucity of uniform items surviving prior to the Napoleonic period, it is quite remarkable how many original red–coats have in fact survived, most being in foreign collections. There are three in the Musée Royal de l'Armée et d'Histoire Militaire, Bruxelles in Belgium, being battalion company coats

of the 9th Foot (East Norfolk) and 26th Foot (Cameronian), plus an unidentified light company coat. There are two in the Musée de l'Empéri, Salon de Provence in France, being battalion company coats of the 26th Foot and 83rd Foot. There is another battalion company coat of the 83rd Foot in the Musée de l'Armée, Les Invalides, Paris. In the Royal Irish Fusiliers Regimental Museum, Armagh there is a grenadier company coat of the 87th Foot (Prince of Wales's Own Irish) and in the collection of the Cape Ann Historical Association, Gloucester, Massachusetts, there is a light company coat of the 104th Foot. What these surviving items prove beyond doubt is that no two are identical, even if from the same regiment, as demonstrated by the subtle but material variations between the two battalion company coats of the 26th Foot and the two from the 83rd Foot. Whilst the precise provenance of these coats is unclear, they are all apparently dated to the period of the Peninsular campaigns, indeed the two 83rd Foot coats are probably both from the second battalion. Yet just the various shape and angle of pockets and chest lace all testify to the fact these items, whilst made to sealed patterns, were constructed in numerous sweat shops throughout Britain and then subject to further alterations by regimental tailors. Indeed, cloth was actually sent straight to the 'Front Line' to be made into clothing at Regimental HQs which could lead to a certain amount of stress particularly when hostilities were on.

The standard soldier's regimental coat was made from a coarse woollen broad-cloth that through felting, and raising the nap, had a smooth surface in which the warp and weft could not be distinguished. The body of the coat was formed from just four pieces, two fronts and two backs, with only two side seams running into the small of the back. This both ensured an awkward fit and a certain looseness in the lower back. This contrasted with the shoulder seams, which, being off the shoulder, resting instead on the shoulder blades, meant the fit around the shoulders was tight, as were the equally closely cut armholes. There was no padding in the shoulder, rather the sleeve followed its natural slope. The sleeves themselves were cut on a curve, being long and narrow, with cuffs just sufficiently wide to admit the soldier's hand. Shoulder straps were made of two pieces of broad-cloth, an underlay of red and a top piece in the facing colour. Here Keith has uncovered one regimental peculiarity of the 33rd in that their shoulder straps were faced in white, not the red of the regimental facings. The shoulder straps were attached so as to slant towards the rear of the shoulder

following the angle of the seam, thus making them less apparent when viewed from the front. For the battalion company coat, a worsted fringe was added at the shoulder seam. Whilst the clothing warrant required a standing collar three inches in height and cuffs three and a half inches in depth, both to be in the regimental facing colour, the surviving coats show significant variations, some collars being as high as four inches. Finally, the coat was distinguished with the respective regimental pattern of woven lace and pewter buttons. The clothing warrants detailed both the coloured stripes and 'worms' that formed the respective regimental patterns and also specified the spacing of loops on the coats front, cuffs and pockets. The shape of the loops could be square-ended, pointed or bastion. As for buttons, the number of which varied with the spacing of regimental lace, but averaged around 30, here regimental tradition and the preference of colonels played a key role. Some were just cast with a regimental number, the 33rd's button having the numeral '33' inside a continuous wreath, whilst others bore elements of regimental emblems, for example the figure of Britannia on those of the 9th Foot (East Norfolk).

To accurately reconstruct one of these coats is obviously not cheap, costing anything in excess of £250. In respect of the cloth, a company that has been supplying the British Army for over 200 years, Abimelech Hainsworth of Pudsey in Leeds, can supply the appropriate woollen broad-cloth for both the body of the coat and facings. It is equally fortunate that a company still operates that has the original machines that can weave the half inch wide regimental lace with the appropriate coloured stripe. By the Napoleonic period all stripes were straight which is fortunate as the cost, both in time and money, prohibits the manufacture of the earlier lines or worms which like their namesake waved or zig-zagged through the lace. Labour was cheap in those days. Although woven lace is not particularly expensive per yard, costs soon mount when it is appreciated that an average coat requires around twelve yards of lace, all of which must be stitched on by hand, particularly the intricate loops on the chest, cuffs and pockets.

As for other items such as the cap or shako, various warrants give some clue as to their construction, though fortunately a number of original shakoes have survived. The Regimental Museum at Halifax possesses an original example worn by an officer at Waterloo. This shako comes complete with bullet hole, the wearer surviving this unexpected ventilation of his cap to write about his experience from Paris during the occupation. From this and other surviving

This posed shot of an NCO of the *21eme* shows how the general cut of French line infantry clothes had changed with the Bardin regulations of 1812. Apparently inspired by the cut of the short-tailed Polish Kurtka, the white plastron style lapels of the blue habit-veste now closed to the waist. The French style of shako had been evolving for some time, a slightly higher, less flared version having been introduced in 1807. Alongside the brass chin-scales, cockade and green company pom-pom, the most distinctive feature of the shako was the stamped brass 'eagle-over-crescent' plate bearing the regimental number. Rather like its British GR counterpart, although there was a regulation pattern in Bardin, many regiments had their own variations for distinction, that of the 21eme being an example. Although the sabre-briquet was no longer issued to the ordinary fusilier, NCOs still carried the Year XI pattern as part of their rank distinction. Chris Durkin.

examples, measurements and other details have been taken enabling an accurate reconstruction of the Belgic shako to be made. The regimental museum permitted patterns to be taken of specific regimental metal items such as buttons, the cross-belt plate and shako plate that served as the basis for the necessary moulds for these items.

Finally, in respect of equipment including leather items, few original items have survived from what must have been quite literally the millions made. Few shoes have survived for example. Those that do, again give clues as to construction, though often called boots, that item of footwear did not officially make an appearance until 1823. Consequently, the specifications found in various warrants and documents combined with detail taken from contemporary prints have proved an important source for reconstruction. For example, using surviving items, information from original documents and period illustrations, particularly one of the 6th Foot (1st Warwickshire Regiment) circa 1802, Keith was able to reconstruct the small cross-strap joining the respective cross-belts at the soldier's rear. The strap prevented the cartridge pouch and bayonet belt from riding forward when a soldier marched or moved. The *33rd* have chosen this system of holding the cross-belts down, while other Redcoats have utilised a belt wrapped around the waist to hold the cross-belts in place. This method also dispels the myth that the cartridge pouch was fixed to a button on the coat's rear. Sixty rounds of cartridge weight would have soon torn the button off.

Facing the indomitable redcoats across the field of battle were the equally determined infantry of Napoleon. Recreating the soldiers who marched from Cadiz to Moscow and as far afield as the Pyramids are

the *21eme Ligne*. Formed in 1978 as a regiment in the *Napoleonic Association*, today the *21eme* is the largest French Napoleonic regiment in Britain, if not Europe and America, with over 130 active members. Dedicated to reconstructing a late Imperial infantry company of the years 1812–15, the *21eme* is proud of the fact that it can perform the contemporary company drill with the appropriate number of troops. Like the *33rd* that reconstructs the ordinary centre company of Wellington's Redcoats, the *21eme* represents an 'average' fusilier company of the French Army.

Researching the clothes and equipment of the Imperial French soldier is generally straight forward. The starting point for the late Empire is the comprehensive regulations of 19 January 1812, named after Major Bardin who was responsible for their issue. In typical Napoleonic style they record every item in exhaustive detail. Next, numerous items have survived in museums in France and in the many nations Napoleon's Grande Armée 'visited'. The most comprehensive collection is in the Musée de l'Armée at Les Invalides, Paris. Here complete uniforms as well as numerous individual items are on display with far more stored in backrooms. Although it can take some effort, it is possible to view those items not on display. Other important collections for the study of Napoleon's soldiers are the Musée Napoléonien de Fontainbleau and the Musée de l'Empéri, Salon-de-Provence. These also have well stocked archives that include both written documents and numerous contemporary illustrations. It is the latter, particularly the paintings of the Otto Manuscript and the drawings of Martinet, that offer evidence for specific regimental distinctions. As with colonels in the British Army, French commanders often ensured their regiment had some form of distinguishing item or style. Whilst the creative interpretation of regulations had been extensive earlier in the Empire, despite the stricter imposition of the 1812 Bardin regulations, there is evidence of continued 'creativity'. Finally, there is a long-standing tradition in France of high quality military artists such as Lucien Rousselot, Albert Rigondaud ('Rigo') and Bucquoy. Today, this is continued in magazines such as *Tradition* that offer superbly illustrated and highly researched articles on every aspect of the French soldier.

Only a few items specific to the *21eme* have survived, a button dated to 1809 is in the small battlefield museum at Aspern-Essling in Austria and the Regimental museum at Canjuers has been of great assistance. Over a decade ago, on a research visit to the Musée de l'Armée, the *21eme* Adjutant, Chris Durkin and senior research officer, Keith Redfern were able to make contact with Colonel Paul Willing, Conservateur at the Musée de l'Armée. He was able to put them in contact with Adolf Leschevin, a senior

Since 1793, British soldiers had fought against the forces unleashed by the French Revolution. Here, the clothes and equipment of the *9eme Légère* reflect the appearance of the Revolution and Directory. Their cut-away deep blue coats and black bicorne hats were highly distinctive. In many ways the 9eme were similar to the 68th in that although classified as specialist light infantry, they were trained to fight in close order alongside line infantry. English Heritage.

By the latter years of the Empire (nearly 20 years later), the appearance of French infantry had greatly changed, the low bicorne replaced by a bell-topped shako and short tailed jacket. Recreating a fusilier company of the *21eme Ligne*, these Imperial soldiers are drawn-up shoulder to shoulder in a manner almost indistinguishable from their British opponents. At the end of the line is the regiment's Eagle, which as the symbol of the Emperor would have been defended to the death. English Heritage.

member of the modern *21eme* regiment's veteran association. Just after the Second World War, the regiment became the *21eme Régiment de Camp* with responsibility for Camp de Canjuers, an enormous French training ground between Nice and Monaco. In 1990 the regiment changed back to being the *21eme de Ligne*, protected from post-Cold War reductions by the unit's antiquity. However, with the forthcoming end to conscription in France and inevitable reductions, the *21eme* fears amalgamation or disbandment, which would just leave the veterans association and the British based *21eme*. Over the years, Adolf Leschevin has willingly offered his time and contacts to ensure the *21eme* has access to all available information on the regiment, and has arranged for the British *21eme* to visit their modern counterparts.

In reconstructing the uniform of the infantry fusilier of 1812–15, the starting point is the shako. The Bardin regulations provide specific dimensions that are confirmed by surviving items. Constructed from heavy duty felt and leather, and embellished with a stamped brass eagle plate, tricolour cockade, white cords and company pom-pom, this is not a light item to wear. However, the bell topped shape ensured the French soldier had a distinctive silhouette that was alluded to by none other than the Duke of Wellington himself. When in 1812 the British light dragoons received a new uniform that included a distinctly 'French' style shako, there were numerous complaints that they had been '…absolutely metamorphosed…to Frenchmen' and to be challenged with comments such 'Who's that damned Frenchman?' However, the year after Waterloo, British infantry exchanged their Belgic shakos for a distinctly bell-topped 'French' version.

The short tailed blue jacket or *habit-veste* with red collar piped blue, white 'plastron'-style lapels piped red, red cuffs piped white, blue flaps and vertical pockets piped red, white turnbacks, blue shoulder straps piped red and brass buttons is undoubtedly the most complex item of uniform to be constructed. Whilst lacking the woven lace of its British

Although the common image of Napoleonic French infantry tactics was the column, they fought in line just as often as the British. The respective drill manuals were identical in concept, the differences being minor variations in arms drill. As illustrated here, French drill manuals taught various methods of delivering fire in line so as to maintain a continuous hail of shot, be it by dividing a line into divisions, wings, etc. The tactic of assaulting in column was meant to be reserved for when the opposing line had been shaken by cannon and was ready to break. Wellington's use of the reverse slope proved an effective counter to this. English Heritage.

counterpart, its narrow blue, red and white piping that frames collar, cuffs, plastron, pockets, turnbacks and shoulder straps requires hours of careful hand stitching. Equally, the slit cuff with cuff flap and three pointed rear pockets require care and attention for accurate reproduction. At least the flap fronted linen overalls and black gaiters offer a fairly straightforward task.

As for leatherwork, as with the shako, alongside the specified dimensions in the regulations, surviving items provide not only confirmation of these, but also the chance to study the construction. The cartridge box in particular needs to be opened if its internal workings are to be reproduced and it is in these cases

that even the most detailed regulations take second place to the study of original artefacts. The fusilier of 1812 had dispensed with a separate shoulder belt for the bayonet, the bayonet frog being attached to the front of the cartridge belt. Again, this highly distinctive manner of carrying the bayonet requires the study of surviving pieces to ensure an accurate reproduction of how the attachment was constructed and worked.

Finally, the musket carried by all French fusiliers was the 1777-pattern 'Charleville', as modified in year IX/XIIII, reproductions of this being fortunately available from various companies. However, care must be taken to acquire the correct model, as Charleville was a generic name similar to 'Brown Bess'. In the same way that the Bess went through various models, the long land, short land, India, etc, so did the Charleville. Although older versions of the 1777-pattern continued to be used right up to Waterloo, whilst not inaccurate to be equipped with the late Republican model for example, the early version in service during the American War of Independence would be stretching a point.

American Civil War

In the history of re-enactment in Britain, it is surprising that one of the first re-enactment groups was dedicated to recreating the American Civil War. For some it seems strange that today around 1,000 Englishmen recreate a war which was by definition fought by Americans, in America on American issues. Be that as it may, 'The War Between the States' has

In America, thousands of re-enactors assemble for some of the commemorative events staged on the actual battlefields, enabling formations to be assembled that operate with authentic numbers. Here, at the Battle of Shiloh, a full company of re-created Confederate infantry advances towards the enemy. Dr Alec Hasenson.

always attracted considerable interest in Europe and has resulted in the formation of a number of historical groups. The first, *The Southern Skirmish Association*, was founded in 1968 and has since been joined by the *American Civil War Society* and various other groups and individual companies.

The question arises as to what it is that so attracts Englishmen to don American uniforms and stage battles that occurred 3,500 miles away. Many American Civil War re-enactors claim to feel a close affinity with the original protagonists as a consequence of our shared Anglo-Celtic ancestry. There may be something in this, but the popularity of American Civil War re-enacting in Germany, Holland, France

and even the Czech Republic suggests there are other influences at work. For Confederates there is the pull of the 'wrong but romantic' lost cause and for both sides there is the fascination of the curious mixture of old-style stand-up fighting and modern military developments. The fact that the political and military leaders of both sides were well known to each other gives the American Civil War an added poignancy. Finally, there is the fascination of the war being the first of the modern industrial age with the first machine guns, percussion grenades, torpedoes, barbed wire, trenches and ironclads.

Another attraction is the rich source of contemporary photographs and original items that allow an exact re-creation of a soldier's kit. In recent years these pictures and surviving artefacts, particularly clothes and leather work, have been subjected to detailed study in the States resulting in the production of increasingly accurate copies of uniforms and accoutrements. Two or three groups in

Alongside infantry, full-size gun batteries are also fielded enabling both participants and members of the public to gain an idea of the impact made by just the noise of so many guns. Again, taken at the Shiloh event, Confederate infantry await the order to advance behind the gun line whilst the artillery softens up the enemy. Dr Alec Hasenson.

England have been able to make good use of this research. Justly renowned for its attention to detail and offering an evocative portrayal of the veterans of Robert E. Lee's army of North Virginia is *Company F, 55th Virginia*. With around 30 members, it offers the best portrayal of Confederate troops this side of the Atlantic. Its objective is not just to reconstruct the appearance of Civil War soldiers but to demonstrate how they ate, slept, marched and, most importantly, how they drilled. Numerous diaries, official records and regulations make it clear that the soldiers of Lee's Army were well trained. Today's *Company F* is proud that it can perform all elements of Civil War line and skirmish drill as contained in Hardee's Tactics.

Although *Company F* mostly concentrates on living history impressions, it does occasionally participate in battle re-enactments when they can join with like-minded company sized groups to perform as a battalion. A favourite is the event staged every other year at Weston Park by the *American Civil War Society*. On these occasions Company F places itself at the disposal of Colonel Murfin's European Battalion, happy to be just another 'brick' in the battalion 'wall'.

Back in 1861, many of the Confederacy's regiments were built around the cadre of existing volunteer formations. Thus it was with the 55th Virginia. Companies C and F of that regiment had been raised

The massed ranks of *Company F, 55th Virginia* reflects the wide variety of clothes worn by all mid-war Confederate units. The nearest soldier is distinguished by his regulation grey frock coat as compared to the various shades of grey of the 'Roundabouts' (Shell Jackets) of the majority. Headgear and trousers are equally varied, many of the former being various styles of slouch hat. Some wear captured Union blue trousers, others civilian brown, grey and 'butternut'. Captain Perry leads the company forward dressed in a high quality blue-grey Roundabout and wearing a regulation grey kepi. Richard O'Sullivan.

as early as 1859 in response to John Brown's raid on Harper's Ferry. Further volunteer companies were added in the spring and summer of 1861 and four more transferred to the unit from the militia to avoid conscription in the spring of 1862. The regiment saw action in many of the great battles of the war including Seven Days, Second Manassas, Fredericksburg, Chancellorsville and Gettysburg. It was virtually destroyed as a fighting unit at the battle of Sayler's Creek on 6 April 1865, leaving just 21 men to surrender with Lee at Appomattox Court House three days later. Company F was recruited under the name of the Essex Sharp Shooters from amongst the wealthy slave owners and gentry of that county. No

fewer than 20 of its 60 members went on to be elected officers in the 55th Virginia. The company was then filled up with less exalted members of the community providing the men re-enacting the unit with an interesting choice of portrayals. All four of the original company's officers were killed at the battle of Frayser's Farm on 30 June 1862 whilst in the act of overrunning a Federal battery.

The members of today's *Company F* chose their unit with care. The service records of the 55th Virginia are remarkably complete and one of its soldiers, a Marylander named Christian Redwood, was a prolific and skilled writer and artist. After the war he returned to Baltimore where he produced no fewer than seven beautifully illustrated accounts of his wartime experiences. These include descriptions of fighting, camping, cooking and leisure pursuits and also contain biographical sketches of three of his company's black servants. The accompanying picture of the 55th attacking the Stone Barn at Gettysburg is one of his more famous works. Many other, usually labelled as general pictures of Confederate soldiers, are portraits of men he fought and lived alongside, a unique record of the 55th at war.

It is one thing though to have pictorial representations of soldiers on campaign, it is quite

This close up of the men of *Company F, 55th Virginia* show them awaiting their Captain's order. Whilst no two soldiers are dressed alike, all have the necessary cartridge pouch and cap box, and all carry clean and serviceable rifled muskets. A company would have drilled each day to ensure it could perform the various evolutions in Hardee's Tactics. Richard O'Sullivan.

another to create physical copies of their clothes and equipment. That this has proved possible is thanks to men like Les Jensen who made use of his time as a researcher at the Museum of the Confederacy in Richmond to make a detailed study of Confederate uniforms. Jensen concluded that the Confederate Quartermaster's Department was much more efficient than has generally been supposed. He discovered that it had succeeded in having huge amounts of cloth manufactured and that this had then been made up into hundreds of thousands of uniforms both in factories and by a small army of outworkers around major supply depots such as Richmond, Atlanta and Columbus. Much of this cloth was quite unlike modern material.

Whilst numerous items of Confederate clothing have survived, it is one thing to reproduce the correct tailoring and cut, but it is another to precisely match the weave of cloth and colour. Modern cloth is quite different in its manufacture from nineteenth century material and it is here that another American, Charlie Childs, a weaver and tailor from Ohio, has elevated the inexact art of Civil War uniform reproduction to almost a precise science. Having studied original items in museums and private collections, he has meticulously copied these in every detail. The study of these surviving garments has established that most were made from one of two kinds of combination cotton and woollen cloth, neither commercially available in the late twentieth century. The first, known then as 'jeans' was a cheap, uncomfortable and not particularly durable cloth long used by farmers and labourers. It was a cotton warp, woollen fill cloth (meaning it had a cotton weave and woollen weft), usually twill. The second was a more refined fabric known as 'satinet'. This was woven in such a way as to hide the cotton in the cloth face – a type of 'poor man's broadcloth'. It was only later in the war that the Confederacy began to import large quantities of blue-grey kersey, a pure woollen twill from Europe. Skilled tailors like Childs and companies like *Past Patterns* now produce detailed patterns enabling keen re-enactors to make accurate copies of a wide variety of these uniforms.

As to the colour of Confederate cloth, much fruitless argument has been expended on this subject. Childs has established that whilst some was indeed regulation grey, the famous 'butternut' was in fact a generic description covering various shades of brown. It was described at the time by David Thompson, a captured Federal soldier of the 9th New York Volunteers, as 'a colour running all the way from deep coffee brown up to the whitish brown of ordinary dust.' For decades, historians have assumed it was the product of homespun cloth dyed with walnut ('butternut') shells. Whilst there is no doubt such homespun did exist, Child's inspection of surviving 'butternut' coloured clothes has proved that most cloth was factory-made, not hand-loomed. Thus, whilst vegetable dyes were used, this was done at the factory. Further, experiments at the University of North Carolina have demonstrated that woollen and woollen-cotton cloth that has been vegetable-dyed grey soon turns brown after a few weeks' exposure to sunlight as vegetable-dyed grey was an unstable dye and had a tendency to oxidise, turning it into a dirty sandy-yellow colour. Thus contemporary eyewitness descriptions of Confederate soldiers wearing grey must be treated with a little caution as they may well have quickly turned a shade of sandy-yellow/brown, that is, butternut. The only significant exception to this would have been the blue-grey kersey imported either as cloth or made up clothes from Britain and Europe.

The men of the present-day *Company F* have adopted a 'mottled', late 1863 to 1864 appearance. Some of their uniforms were hand sewn by Charlie Childs himself, albeit for a price. Cut from hand woven cloth, be it jeans, satinet or kersey, Childs supplies jackets either in kit form for those who feel they can sew for around £100 or already hand stitched

Sitting in the classic 'studio' pose, this soldier of *Company F, 55th Virginia* wears an almost regulation outfit. He has a grey kepi, nine button Roundabout and trousers, along with the standard Brogans. Typically he wears a mix of equipment, a captured Union black waist belt with cap pouch and brass buckle but a Southern-made brown cartridge box and belt. Along with many soldiers on both sides he is armed with a British manufactured Enfield rifled musket. Richard O'Sullivan.

This studio shot shows a soldier in anything but a regulation outfit. Apart from his Enfield musket and the cartridge box, he wears civilian clothes. By 1864 an increasing proportion of Confederate soldiers were reliant on their own clothes, although few actually went barefoot and despite stories, there was never a serious shortage of weapons or ammunition. Richard O'Sullivan.

for around £150. A pair of matching hand-stitched trousers comes in at around £100. These prices reflect the fact that although much of the original cloth was mass produced in factories, today none can produce woven cloth that is accurate, thus all that Childs uses is woven on hand-looms. Other uniforms were machine made by a fine company known as the *Quartermaster Shop* run by Jeff O'Donnell in Michigan and some were made for them by an American comrade in Germany. Their First Sergeant's mother, made at least half of *Company F*'s uniforms, from a pattern in Mike Thomas' *Confederate Sketchbook*.

Good reproduction headgear, particularly the commonly worn slouch hat, is extremely difficult to obtain. Richard O'Sullivan, a long serving member of *Company F*, points out that the majority of slouch hats worn by re-enactors bear little resemblance to those in contemporary photographs. These show most slouch hats worn by Confederate soldiers as stylish with a good shape, not the shapeless versions worn by many

Laid out for inspection, this Confederate soldier is fortunate in having such a complete set of equipment, albeit almost all of it are captured Union items. Certainly the waist belt with cap pouch and bayonet, alongside the cartridge box, falls into the latter category. This is equally true of the canteen, backpack and blue greatcoat. Richard O'Sullivan.

re-enactors today that have more in common with the sort of thing sported by 'Paddington Bear'. This is not just a matter of cut, a good quality felt that retains its shape after numerous soakings is equally important. Most felts available today would have been classified as 'shoddy' in the nineteenth century. Even if they do not dissolve in the rain they soon become shapeless blobs. Fortunately, good quality kepis are available from *Company F*'s American colleagues in Germany.

Good quality reproduction shoes, 'brogans', leatherwork and tin wear is available from an American supplier, *Jarnagin & Co.*, a company operating out of Corinth, Mississippi. Again, utilising surviving items in museums and private collections, as well as contemporary patterns, exact replicas can be purchased off the shelf. This is also true of percussion muskets. The preferred weapon of *Company F* is the 1858 Pattern 'long Enfield' often termed today the three-band Enfield. Proofed originals can still be found. The finest reproductions are manufactured by a British company called Parker Hale and cost about £500. Fine copies are also available from Euroarms of Italy for about £350. Regrettably Indian versions are not suitable as they are several inches too short and have smooth-bore sights.

To add depth and distinction to their impression, *Company F* has had a few special items made up that

reflect the considerable quantities of equipment shipped to the Confederacy from Britain. With the assistance of Alan Larsen, a cobbler in Northampton has produced some pairs of 1861 British Army pattern brogans. With access to an expert tinsmith a number of British Army 'D' Mess Tins have been made, each having an inner tray. Finally, thanks to research by Ron Field in the Virginia Historical Society library, *Company F* is reconstructing the ante-bellum uniform

Right.

Unlike many of his men, Captain Perry of *Company F, 55th Virginia* clearly wears a military uniform. His nine button blue-grey Roundabout is well-tailored and is smartly set off by his red silk sash, whilst his belt buckle displays the seal of Virginia. These items, like his grey kepi and sword, would all have been privately purchased. However, like many of his men, he wears a pair of captured Union blue trousers. Richard O'Sullivan.

Below.

In the field, Captain Perry camped alongside his men, although unlike them, he was not obliged to share a tent. At the back of the tent is a wooden trunk for his personal possessions whilst he has laid out extra clothing, his canteen and other miscellaneous items. Whilst the folding table and chair are plain wood, there is a touch of home comfort on the floor in the guise of a small red carpet. Richard O'Sullivan.

Top.

Most soldiers spent their life between marching and camping, punctuated by the occasional moment of combat. This is a typical scene from a Confederate camp showing soldiers of *Company F, 55th Virginia* relaxing. The simple tent in the foreground is just a piece of canvas supported on a string between two poles. Whilst straw provides the floor, a civilian blanket is draped over, drying out from the previous night. Richard O'Sullivan.

Left.

Specially made for the 55th, this British 'D' Mess Tin reflects the enormous amount of equipment supplied to both sides, courtesy of British industry. However, the soldiers of the 55th who received such items would consider themselves fortunate-most of their compatriots had to make do with a tin mug and plate. James Sykes.

of the Essex Sharp shooters. This includes a cadet grey frock coat, grey shako with black pom-pom and white linen summer wear trousers. The shakos are made by Geoff Toyer, in Northampton.

Whilst Lee's veterans were winning immortality in the fields of Virginia, Maryland and Pennsylvania, far to the west a gruelling and far less glamorous campaign was being fought along the Mississippi and

As with the Confederate units in the States, entire Union regiments can be fielded at the larger commemorative re-enactments. Here a full scale regiment awaits orders at the Gettysburg event, the largest battle re-enactment ever staged with around 12,000 participants. Dr Alec Hasenson.

in Tennessee. From the bitterly fought battle of Shiloh in 1862 through to Sherman's blitzkrieg through the south in 1864/65, the war in the west was of a different nature to that in the east. Rather than being essentially limited to the area between Washington and Richmond, the war in the west spanned hundreds of miles. Further, it can be argued that it was the western campaigns that won the Union the war. For while Lee succeeded in defeating outright or fighting to a halt every Union army sent against him, in the west, Union soldiers ultimately swept the field. They cut the Confederacy in half when they captured the seemingly impregnable bastion of Vicksburg in July 1863 and then, having effectively destroyed Hood's Army of Tennessee, they cut the heart out of the Confederacy in Sherman's ruthless March to the Sea.

The average Union soldier of the western armies offered a stark contrast to the neat and tidy soldiers of the east. Whilst the Army of the Potomac, given its crucial task of defending Washington received priority

in terms of clothes and equipment, Union armies in the west were often ragged and reliant on captured Confederate supplies. It was not unusual until quite late in the war for Union soldiers in the west to find their enemy had better weapons. Equally, whilst the Union soldier in the east spent much of his time in camp between the hard fought but relatively short duration campaigns against Lee, his counterpart marched thousands of miles back and forth across Tennessee and the Mississippi. Recreating these hard marching and fighting troops are the *18th Missouri*, members of the *Southern Skirmish Association*.

The original 18th were formed in Northern Missouri at the commencement of the conflict. On 13 November 1861, various disparate companies of volunteers were brought together and mustered into the service of the United States under the designation the 18th Regiment Missouri Volunteer Infantry. When they subsequently reported to the Instructional Depot at Benton Barracks in Missouri in February 1862, their colonel reported that his 705 men were ragged, with few uniforms and armed with a mixture of Enfields, Austrian and Springfield muskets (many the private property of the men).

The *18th* was eventually fully equipped for the field and saw the first of its many hard fights at Shiloh in April 1862 as part of Prentiss' Division. It went on to fight in the subsequent campaigns with the Army of the Tennessee. Rather than being disbanded when the term of its original volunteers was concluded, many soldiers re-enlisted as Veteran Volunteers in early 1864 ensuring the 18th served throughout the conflict in the west. It thus concluded its service with Sherman in the Carolinas at the Battle of Bentonville and the surrender of General Johnston with the remains of the Confederate Army of Tennessee at Raleigh in May 1865.

Today's reactivated formation represents Company E of the 18th. It was raised in 1984, principally inspired by the text of Professor Leslie Ander's history of the regiment (published by Bobbs Merrill in 1968). The main aim of the *18th* is to give as accurate an impression as possible of the Federal soldier in the western theatre of the American Civil War during the

Displaying a far greater degree of uniformity as compared to their Confederate opponents, these Union troops reflect the North's industrial power. The soldiers here are from the Army of the Potomac as they appeared at Gettysburg in July 1863 (fielded for the Gettysburg event). Given the proximity of Washington DC, throughout the war the soldiers in the eastern theatre received priority in supply, ensuring a far greater regularity in clothes and equipment. Conversely, their western compatriots came a decided second. Dr Alec Hasenson.

middle part of 1863, both on active campaign and in fixed encampments, in particular the Army of the Tennessee characterised by its looser discipline yet strong fighting spirit, and greater variety in uniform and general appearance.

Researching the *18th* beyond the text of Anders book has proved difficult as many of the regiment's original records were lost in a major fire. However, much has been gleaned from the *Official Records of the War of Rebellion*, histories of other Missouri Volunteer regiments and the study of many photographs of individuals, groups and regiments, both studio and candid. Indeed, members of the *18th* have unearthed photographs of the 18th not published in Anders' official history. The members have also drawn upon the vast amount of independent research carried out by fellow re-enactors and amateur historians both in Britain and America, and are in contact with their sister companies of the *18th* in the States and Germany. Despite this, the First Sergeant (described as the 'general manager' of the company in Kautz's 1864 book *Customs of Service*) of Company E, Colin Wright, is at pains to stress that there is no real way of knowing precisely what the unit truly wore during any particular period of the war, rather the *18th* aims for as accurate an 'impression' as possible.

In reconstructing the uniform of the 18th the

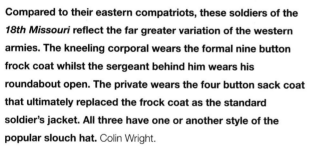

Compared to their eastern compatriots, these soldiers of the *18th Missouri* reflect the far greater variation of the western armies. The kneeling corporal wears the formal nine button frock coat whilst the sergeant behind him wears his roundabout open. The private wears the four button sack coat that ultimately replaced the frock coat as the standard soldier's jacket. All three have one or another style of the popular slouch hat. Colin Wright.

It is possible that this *18th Missouri* sergeant's roundabout began life as a regulation frock coat but has had its skirt removed as an encumbrance. Like the corporal, he wears the standard set of regulation equipment, although he sports a privately purchased civilian slouch hat. Unlike the corporal and possibly reflecting his higher rank, he is armed with a model 1863 number 4 pattern Enfield Rifled Musket. Colin Wright.

foundation document is the *Regulations for the Uniform and Dress of the Army of the United States – 1861*, issued by the War Department. This is then tempered by the various sources indicated above and what is known of the items available at the various arsenals supplying the soldiers at any particular time. Like the *55th Virginia*, the *18th* obtains many of its uniform items and weapons from the numerous suppliers and merchants that serve the American Civil War re-enactment scene. In this respect the sheer scale of American Civil War re-enactment ensures significant economies of scale.

As with the rest of the Federal Army, the regulation coat for an infantryman was the dark blue single-breasted 'frock' coat with a skirt extending half the distance to the knee. Surviving examples show the cloth of these coats was normally cut raw at the hem of the skirt whilst only the upper body of the coat was lined. Numerous photographs and surviving items prove though that various other styles of coat were worn, most common being the Shell Jacket or 'Roundabout'. Originally derived from Frock Coats that had had the skirt removed, this evolved into a specific garment. Reflecting its origins this short jacket had nine buttons down the front and two on each cuff. The Fatigue Jacket was also popular being described as a four-button 'sack' coat. Originally the Fatigue Jacket had been issued as the soldier's working jacket along with the Frock Coat for more formal occasions. As the war progressed this became the soldier's standard coat, replacing the Frock Coat. The version of the Fatigue Jacket the 18th received was the Cincinnati Arsenal Pattern, characterised by a mix of machine and hand stitching, a lining and an inside left pocket.

At the start of the war the four-button sack coat was purely for fatigue duty. As the war progressed it quickly replaced the frock coat as the standard infantry coat. Again, like his NCO, this private of the *18th Missouri* has almost a full set of equipment, although he wears a rolled waxed oilskin poncho over his left shoulder. Like the corporal, his slouch hat probably began life as a regulation Hardee Hat. Unlike the two NCOs, he is armed with an American manufactured weapon, the model 1861 Springfield Rifled Musket. Colin Wright.

This side view of the corporal clearly shows the cartridge box with its brass US plate and the arrangement of the various belts. Equally clear is the corporal's waxed (for waterproofing) backpack in which all personal items as well as extra clothes had to be carried. If unlucky, at night the blanket rolled on top of the pack would be his only cover. Colin Wright.

Regulations specified the 'Hardee Hat' for headgear, this being made of black felt with a crown six and a quarter inches in height and a brim of three and a quarter inches wide, turned up on one side. Like the fatigue jacket, the forage cap had originally been issued alongside the Hardee Hat as a working cap. Similar to, yet distinct from the eastern theatre Kepi, the forage cap had a high welted pasteboard crown. Again, photographic evidence reveals a prevalence of non-regulation headgear that was 'foraged', privately purchased or supplied from home. Western soldiers appear to have favoured a brimmed hat of some description to cope with the dual torments of broiling sun and torrential rain. In the early months of the *18th Missouri's* service this was in fact their Hardee's, the turned up brim of which was flattened out to resemble the slouch hat.

Unlike clothes, the black leather accoutrements, boots and ancillary items tended to be fairly standard. The former included a waist belt with a lead backed stamped brass oval 'US' buckle. A cap box was carried on the right of this waist belt with a lambs wool insert to help prevent caps falling out, whilst the bayonet was carried in a frog on the left. Cartridge boxes were US Model 1855 with space for forty cartridges and including another lead backed stamped brass 'US' oval fitted to the flap to act as a weight. The cartridge box was suspended by a sling over the left shoulder that had a lead backed stamped brass 'Eagle' plate affixed to it. As for boots, the Jefferson Brogan style was universal to both sides, which along with the leather accoutrements and ancillary items such as the 1858 pattern canteen, the haversack and knapsack, tin plate and cup/boiler, knife, fork and spoon, can all be obtained from commercial suppliers.

During a brief halt on the march, a corporal has divested himself of his equipment to gain access to his pack, taking advantage of the stacked muskets to hang his belts from. Among the items of extra clothes, he has a small packet of coffee beans that he is about to draw on to put in the tin mug by his side. Once water was added, this would be heated over an open fire for an early form of instant coffee. Colin Wright.

During its service, the 18th carried two types of musket. Between 1862 and early 1864 it carried the .69 calibre Model 1842 Springfield Musket. These were smooth bore muskets fitted with a percussion lock. Then, in early 1864 when the 18th re-enlisted as Veteran Volunteers, the men were issued with the new model .58 calibre 1861 Springfield Rifled Musket. For today's 18th, both these weapons have presented problems as it is only recently that an American made reproduction Model 1842 Musket has become available in Britain. Although the Model 1861 has been available, because it is rifled weapon, a part one firearms certificate is required to hold it. The only alternative if it is to be held on a shotgun certificate is for it to be re-bored to a smoothbore, which then requires re-proofing, adding considerable expense to the item. Thus, due to economic and practical pressures the *18th* has been compelled to depart from

absolute accuracy, and whilst a few members do possess Springfields, the majority have, in substitution, the smoothbore reproduction Enfield Model 1853 Number 4 Pattern rifled musket. As very great numbers of this weapon were exported to both sides in the war it is not an inaccurate weapon in the generic sense. It is though the intention of the *18th*, now reproduction Model 1842 muskets are becoming available to progressively re-equip with this weapon.

In conclusion, there is an interesting link between the 18th and the next great American conflict. Its first muster in November 1861 was held in the town of Laclede, Linn County, Missouri where one of the shopkeepers sold his shop in order to enlist. The man who purchased the shop was one John Fletcher Pershing, whose infant son stood by his side to watch the 18th march off to war, one John J. Pershing. Years later he too joined the army, rising to command its troops in Mexico and Flanders 1916–18, and ultimately, the entire United States Army.

World Wars One and Two

With twentieth century reconstructions, there is an overwhelming body of evidence. Much if not all the clothes, equipment and weapons can be obtained as actual originals. Consequently, in seeking to reconstruct a particular soldier, whether a First World War American Doughboy or British Tommy, or a Second World War member of the Wehrmacht, it is not so much about discovering evidence as selecting it. Further, from amongst the numerous surviving artifacts, it is often more a decision as to how items were worn, or even if they were, than discovering how they were manufactured.

British re-enactment is justly renowned for its enormous variety – just about anything that can be recreated is, including many foreign contingents, particularly the flourishing American Civil War groups alongside other familiar American conflicts: the French and Indian Wars 1755–60 and the American War of Independence 1775–83. However, a new group now recreates possibly the least known of the North American Continent's conflicts General Pershing's Punitive Expedition into Mexico of 1916.

In 1911, the pro-American Mexican dictator Diaz was overthrown. He was succeeded by a series of short-lived and chaotic regimes. The ongoing political chaos resulted in a profusion of bandit groups who occasionally slipped over the Rio Grande into the United States. The American government responded to these frontier incidents and an 'insult to the flag' when the crew of the USS *Dolphin* was arrested in Tampico on 9 April 1914, by occupying Veracruz from 21 April to 23 November. However, the border incursions continued and culminated on 9 March 1916 when Pancho Villa led over 2500 'Villistas' into New Mexico. Some 700 of these bandits stormed into the small town of Columbus, charging down the main street shooting anything that moved and throwing grenades into any open doorway. As the Villistas retired back to Mexico, the tiny 29 man garrison of Columbus under Colonel Frank Tomkins bravely gave

pursuit, ultimately chasing Villa back over the Rio Grande (this act of reckless bravery made Tomkins a national hero). However, President Woodrow Wilson had had enough and within days, on 15 March, General Pershing was ordered across the border with ten thousand men to capture Villa and end the bandit threat. This 'Punitive Expedition' lasted for nine months, only withdrawing on 30 January 1917. While Villa remained free and the military actions that resulted were not an unmitigated success for American arms, it did ultimately deter further serious incursions.

Now whilst this historic footnote might not seem the most likely event to recreate for British re-enactors, *Pershing's Doughboys* do just that, and with almost entirely original clothes and equipment. Formed in the mid-1990s by Duncan Aran and his brother, the group now has around two dozen members. Duncan and his brother have been collectors of militaria for 12 years, having long ago concentrated on American pieces. Duncan originally began re-enacting with a Wild West group, then joined the *American Civil War Society* and the *14th Brooklyn* (more accurately the 14th New York State Militia). Intrigued by the period of military history that witnessed the final transition from Napoleonic tactics to modern, the Punitive Expedition became the focus of study. Here, Mexicans armed with a mixture of Mauser bolt action rifles, lever action Winchesters, Marlin Carbines and Colt single action pistols (mostly obtained from nefarious American sources) fought a modern mobile guerrilla war. They confronted American troopers still armed with sabres, yet also sporting model 1911 Colt automatic pistols and Springfield 1903 model bolt action rifles. Alongside the traditional cavalry troopers, the American Army for the first time utilised motorised transport for supplies and the fledgling Air service in the form of eight Curtis-Wright bi-planes. General Pershing himself was driven around in a Dodge command car by non-other than the young Lieutenant George C.

Whilst cavalry had been all but removed from the European battlefield by 1916, the wide open expanse of the Mexican-American border and a distinct lack of trenches and barbed wire ensured they continued to play a crucial role. This picture displays a recreated 1st Lieutenant and sergeant of American cavalry as they would have appeared during Pershing's 1916 Punitive Expedition. All the clothes and equipment being worn are original. Duncan Arun.

As with the life of all soldiers, mundane work details rather than glorious charges filled most of their waking hours, even during Pershing's Punitive Expedition. Here a 1st Lieutenant of the Quartermaster corps is detailing some men to clean out the stables. Despite this being the age of mass production, no two soldiers are dressed alike, a mixture of M1910 Service coats (cotton canvas), and M1910 canvas breeches being worn. The soldier at the centre of the three wears a rare rifle belt with the early 'rimless eagle snap' closure typical of the early stages of the Punitive Expedition. Duncan Arun.

Patton, his adjutant.

Having studied the Punitive Expedition for over a decade and amassed a remarkable collection of original pieces, by the mid-1990s it seemed the logical thing to do more than just display these at home. With others from the *14th Brooklyn* and *American Civil War Society*, the group was formed with the object of utilising almost entirely original clothes and equipment. To successfully achieve this has been no small feat, both in terms of contacts and money. Utilising both traditional catalogues, but increasingly the enormous range of contacts available on the Internet, the mail order dealers in the States have done much business. Given that Pershing's Punitive Expedition was immediately followed by American involvement in the First World War, the group also undertakes an American Great War impression. For this and the

Pershing impression, the numerous World War One discussion groups on the Internet have often been able to assist with questions over the identity of existing pieces of equipment and locating those still required.

Dressed as a cavalry First Lieutenant, Duncan's 1912 model officer's garrison cap made in Kalamazoo, Michigan cost over £150. Better made than trooper's caps and with the tan band that indicates it is an officer's, Duncan was lucky to find one that fitted, given that it has a stiff basket inside. His 1912 model cotton-canvas service coat is the unlined summer version. The dark bronze finish brass buttons are attached by rings to make them easy to remove and launder the coat. As it is for field wear, there are no metal rank distinctions although the braid on the cuffs

By 1918, several hundred thousand American soldiers had arrived in Northern France. These Doughboys all wear the M1917 steel helmet with its brown leather straps that distinguish it from the post-war and Second World War US type M1917A1, which had a canvas chin strap. All wear issue service respirators at the 'ready' position. These gas mask bags differed from the British type in that they closed at the top with two Lift the Dot (LTD) fasteners. The opening for the respirator bag is worn against the chest as per US Regulation so the bag did not fill up with soil and water in case the men had to crawl along the ground, thus rendering the respirator inoperative. The soldiers are all armed with the regulation M1903 Springfield rifle chambered for the .30.06 cartridge, although due to shortages, many Doughboys went to France with the M17 version. Duncan Arun.

indicate the wearer's commissioned status. Including insignia, this coat cost £100 thus indicating that there were far more surplus coats at the end of 1918 than caps. The 1912 model cotton-canvas breeches cost £40 whilst the 1917 cotton-canvas gaiters cost £25. Gaiters worn are in fact infantry ones, those for the cavalry being lined on the inside with leather (Duncan possess two pairs of the latter, but both are too big for him to wear). His boots are modern reproductions, as original Pershing boots cost at least £400 and cannot

be worn (almost all footwear in the group is reproduction). The belt is a garrison belt, only worn by enlisted personnel in garrison but by officers on campaign. A 1912 Garrison belt can cost £200, hence the one worn by Duncan is a reproduction. In the European theatre of war, Pershing ordered his officers to wear British Sam Brown belts to distinguish them from enlisted personnel as the Americans had no counter-part, just Garrison belts. The holster is a very scarce 1912 swivel hanger (the later World War Two holsters hung directly from the belt), the holster costing over £220 and the hanger £15. His canvas pouch for two spare clips was made by Anson Mills, that worn being the 1917 version costing £20. The much scarcer 1915 version with eagle stamped poppers can cost in excess of £200. Another leather pouch is for a five-round stripper clip for the Springfield rifle. Finally, he wears an original 1911 model colt automatic pistol in the holster made in 1917, although due to the recent Firearms (Amendment) Act, it has had to be deactivated.

When Duncan's brother is uniformed as a sergeant he wears a 1911 campaign hat with yellow hat cords (yellow for cavalry, blue for infantry and red for artillery) cost over £250. His original Wilson goggles were £100 and would have originally been a private army purchase as there was no official equivalent. The wool-cotton mix mid-brown service shirt with elbow re-enforcement is of a pullover design with just a three-button slit down to mid-chest level. This cost between £60-70. A hanger on the right side for a sabre distinguishes the campaign pistol belt; it cost £35. His holster is original, costing between £260 and £350. The revolver in the holster is a Colt 45 New Service model made in 1910 (the last patent date for this model was 1884). However, an American Army, starved of resources over the previous decades, carried many such obsolete weapons. Again, it is deactivated. He carries 1917 US Army Field glasses, costing anything between £70 and £300. His breeches, gaiters and boots are as for the officer. Both the lieutenant

and sergeant wear original lanyards.

As a general comment, Duncan is often intrigued to discover which original items are and are not readily available. For example, the canvas covered scabbard for the 'Bolo' knife that was standard issue to medics and machine gunners seems to be very common and in mint condition, cost as little as £10 each. However, if they have the knife the pair can cost as much as £200 and are fairly rare. Whilst it seems strange that there are so many scabbards in excellent condition but not knives, presumably the answer is that the original contract for the former was never cancelled. A further example of this are the canvas bags, which were designed and made for the 'Pedersen

This Engineer Private First class wears the M1907 Springfield bayonet housed on the left hand side of the M1910 field equipment haversack in a canvas covered leather scabbard (given its rarity the bayonet and scabbard are more expensive than the Springfield rifle). The division badge on the left shoulder is that of the 'First Army' with a red castle to indicate the wearer's branch of service as an engineer. Although out of sight, on his right arm a round 'Engineer specialist' badge (a castle) was worn. Rather than the M1910 canvas leggings worn on the Mexican border, he wears 'Wrap Arounds' that were identical to British Puttees. *Duncan Arun.*

The Great War witnessed women serving in uniform as a recognised element within the armed forces as telephone operators, secretaries, ambulance drivers, Salvation Army helpers and, back in America, the Home Defence Force. Whilst there was no officially issued uniform for women serving with the US forces, it was extremely common for them to make their own that resembled the men's. Here, the woman standing wears the work utility uniform made from chocolate brown cotton canvas whilst her hat is a US regulation chocolate brown 'Daisy Mae'. The armband is 'AEF Salvation Army'. The woman sitting at the switchboard wears the unofficial uniform of the Stateside women's Home Defence Force. *Duncan Arun.*

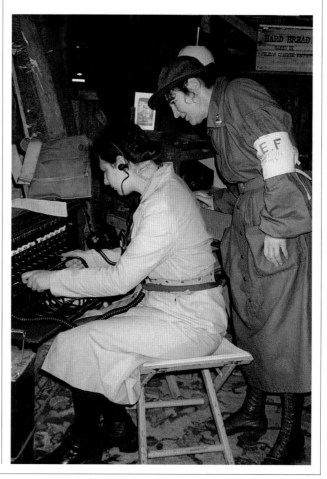

Device' for use with the 1903 Springfield Rifle Mark 1. The Pedersen adaption device, fitted to the standard Springfield, was designed to convert the bolt action rifle into a semi-automatic weapon thus increasing the rate of fire whilst crossing No Mans Land between the trenches. Although the war ended before the Pedersen system saw action, Remington had manufactured over 65,000 such devices. Specialised canvas bags for the infantryman to carry the Pedersen magazines and Springfield bolts were also produced. According to the military records, as the whole device was scrapped as unnecessary at the end of the war, all but a handful were destroyed. However, it seems that the companies who had the contract to manufacture the accessory bags did not cease manufacture and it is very common to find these canvas bags dated 1919 or 1920, mostly in mint condition given they were never used.

Yet another example is the canvas belt for those armed with the Browning Automatic Rifle (BAR). This had a steel cup riveted onto the right hand side for the stock of the BAR to fit into to enable the rifle to be fired from the hip whilst still slung on its sling around the rifleman's neck. Again, the purpose of this was to make it easier to provide increased firepower whilst crossing No Man's Land. The rifleman's belt with the metal cup is quite common, costing around £20 for one dated to 1918. However, the associated bandoleers to hold the magazines are far rarer, as are the suspenders (Braces) to hold the belt up. Duncan suspects that the items that could be utilised were all used by the Army until they were superseded or exhausted from the Quartermaster's store. Many First World War dated web equipment pieces were issued right into the Second World War and in particular

Given the demands of war, members of the AEF Salvation Army inevitably found themselves ever closer to the front-line. Here a young trumpeter looks grateful for the freshly cooked food being prepared so near to the Front. As with so much else utilised in the reconstructions of the Doughboys, all items including the tins of food and cocoa powder are original. Duncan Arun.

Back in August and September 1914, soldiers of the BEF 'The Old Contemptibles' had fought the Germans to a standstill. Here, a lance corporal of the 2nd Manchester's appears, as he would have done at Mons. He wears the pre-war regulation field uniform including the khaki 1902 Pattern Service Dress jacket and 1908 Pattern Webb equipment. As yet the steel helmet was a thing of the future hence he wears the 1902 Pattern Service dress cap known as the 'cheese cutter'. He is in the process of inserting a fresh clip into the magazine of his trusty .303 Lee Enfield. Geoff Carefoot.

Before the outbreak of the Great War, all sides expected combat to be at close quarters. Great stress was laid upon the bayonet. Here, soldiers of the Middlesex Regiment train in a 1914 summer camp in the full pre-war 1902 khaki field service dress for infantry, including back packs. This was not an item a soldier would realistically wear if action was to be engaged with the bayonet, however, in the event there were to be few occasions for the issue to arise. English Heritage.

many BAR ammunition belts were re-worked. Whilst there were slight changes in the method of construction, fundamentally they were made from parts that are stamped with World War I dates. Generally this was very common in the inter-war period, as funding for the American Armed Forces was not exactly a number one priority for the Government. Only items that could not be put to good use and were thus still in the Quartermaster's store would eventually find their way into the Government surplus area and hence end up in collections.

Original officers' uniforms of any type are very scarce. As a rule, as far as the rank and file uniform items go, the cotton canvas types, such as those used in Mexico, are cheaper than the 1912, 1917 or 1918 wool models used in Europe. This is particularly due to the fact that there is more demand from collectors for the European wool items given the greater interest in First World War than in Mexico. Equally, cotton uniforms were worn mainly in garrison and in America whilst seeing very limited service in Europe. The corresponding wool items meanwhile deteriorated rapidly in the trenches of the Western front. As a result there are more cotton uniform items available in good condition even though far more wool ones were made.

Given the group is mostly uniformed in original pieces and lacking any Mexican bandits or the First World War Germans to fight, the *Doughboys* concentrate on living history and commemorative events. This use of original items also means that the group does not represent any specific unit. It is felt, rightly I think most would agree, that to remove original badges and insignia to conform to a chosen unit would be a sacrilege. Recreating a variety of soldiers, the group was honoured last year by being asked to participate by the First Infantry Division (the Big Red One) at the unveiling of the monument to American soldiers at Caumont L'Evente in Normandy. This raised a few eyebrows when the American servicemen present realised that the 'American' Second World War soldiers were in fact British,

As the war progressed, the steel helmet made its appearance. Here, a junior NCO of the 2nd Manchester's and Middlesex pose in camp behind the lines as they would have appeared around the time of the Battle of the Somme in July 1916. Demonstrating the enormous difficulties of equipping the hundreds of thousands of volunteers who had flocked to the colours of 'Kitchener's Army', the lance corporal on the right of the picture has been issued with the substitute set of brown leather webbing. This 1914 pattern webbing resembled the late nineteenth century Slade-Wallace set. Geoff Carefoot.

By 1917–18, earlier shortages had been overcome and new weapons were making an appearance to meet the demands of Trench Warfare. These two junior NCO of the 2nd Manchesters are both 'Bombers'. The lance corporal has the special canvas harness for carrying up to a dozen Mills bombs and wears the small cloth grenade symbol on his upper right arm below his divisional symbol. The corporal has two stick grenades worn in his webbing. Geoff Carefoot.

commemorating their dead at a French monument. They have also commemorated Pershing's men at the only monument to them in Britain at the United States Second World War cemetery at Brookwood in Surrey.

The Doughboys have established strong links with the Columbus Historical Society and the curator of the small museum there in New Mexico to the Punitive Expedition, Marrion Elliot. Amazed that British re-enactors would recreate the little known soldiers of 1916, she has offered every assistance.

When the original Doughboys began arriving in Flanders in late 1917 they passed the muddy veterans of Haig's British Army. By this point in the conflict, the British had learnt many hard lessons about warfare in the twentieth century and the brutal tactic of frontal assault had finally concluded after the slaughter at Passchendaele. Rather, 1918 witnessed the dawn of new tactics and weapons on both sides, the techniques of infiltration by the Germans, the effective co-ordination of tanks, close artillery support and even aircraft by the British, that restored mobility to warfare. In many respects the campaigns of 1918 foreshadowed those of the Second World War rather than the terrible attrition of the preceding three years.

Regardless of this, the abiding image of the First World War is of muddy trenches, barbed wire and the grim tactics of attrition, although given Germany's demand for their 1914 September Programme as the basis for peace until late 1918, it is difficult to see how peace could have been an option. Whether the First World War is considered a senseless slaughter or a terrible but unavoidable conflict to contain Germany, none question the bravery and sacrifice of the ordinary soldiers in the front line. It is their memory and lives that are brought vividly to life by one of Britain's most respected living history groups, *The Great War Society*. The *GWS* was formed on the 70th anniversary of Britain's entry into the First World War on 4 August 1984. Most of the original members were already Napoleonic re-enactors who had discovered that they had a mutual interest in the First World War. Many were already collectors of uniforms and equipment

Marching through the Normandy Bocage, these khaki-clad ***British infantry*** **of June-August 1944 are recognisably the descendants of their 1916–18 forbears. The steel helmet was little changed from 1916, and they are still armed with the .303 Lee Enfield, albeit a later model. However, the style of their clothes had altered considerably, the 1902 Pattern service dress had been replaced in 1940 by a more serviceable Battledress Blouse. Equally, ankle gaiters have replaced the puttees. It is a testament to the serviceability of these changes that the German Model 1944 Field Blouse radically broke with traditional German styles by adopting a design almost identical to the British Battledress Blouse. When worn with the tapered 1942 pattern** *Tuchose* **(trousers) and** *Gamaschen* **(web anklets), the late war German soldier's clothes took on a distinctly British style.** English Heritage.

from the conflict and, motivated by a belief that the ordinary British soldier of the First World War had been neglected, they founded the *GWS*.

When first formed, there was a conscious decision not to recreate any of the specialised or elite formations given the desire to portray the everyday experience of the ordinary British 'Tommy' of the Great War. Rather, with most of the initial members living in the south east, they opted to represent just a single unit, the fourth battalion of the Middlesex Regiment. This formation was chosen as it was a standard county regiment, many of whose battalions served throughout the war in the trenches of the Western Front. The fourth battalion was chosen as it was one of the Regiment's battalions of regulars who fought right through the war from Mons to the Armistice, thus enabling members to represent the British soldier throughout the war. As the society grew and it gained members in the north, the Manchester Regiment was added. Initially the members of the Manchester Regiment alternated their identity between several of its battalions depending upon the nature of the event. However today they represent the eighth battalion, as this was one of the Manchester's battalions of territorials and like the fourth battalion of the Middlesex Regiment, they served right through the conflict from beginning to end.

This close-up of a lance corporal of the Military Police sitting comfortably at the wheel of a jeep shows how serviceable was the new style of battle-dress. Given he proudly sports his red cap, this must be in camp, safely behind the lines. Alongside the MP is the Bren gun, a crucial weapon able to provide a high volume of firepower at close quarters. English Heritage.

Whilst the battalion identities allow the members to represent the soldier throughout the war, it does mean that the members require various changes of clothes and equipment to enable them to accurately represent the evolution of the British soldier's appearance during the conflict. However, by just reconstructing two specific regiments, it does help narrow the focus for research in the enormous body of material available on the First World War. Much time is spent in the various archives studying photographs, documents and early newsreel, and this is compared to surviving items in collections. In this pursuit, many of the smaller provincial museums have proven to be rich sources of information. Equally, as many of the members are collectors much time and effort is spent at militaria fairs and the like, both in further research and in obtaining original items.

Whilst original pieces are available, most are expensive, in fragile condition, and normally not the right size. Unlike the American Army, that allowed its soldiers to take most of their kit home with them at the end of the war, British soldiers were obliged to hand all their clothes back, the only item they were commonly allowed to keep being their greatcoat. Inevitably these uniforms were re-issued until they fell apart, thus making original British First World War items scarce. Consequently, whilst *Pershing's Doughboys* have the option of obtaining original clothes that can still be used, the members of the *GWS* must mostly opt for modern reconstructions. One major advantage they have over earlier periods, however, is that by the nineteenth and twentieth century, there were official 'sealed patterns', essentially model items that manufacturers were required to copy for any military contract. Most of those for the First World War have survived and are available for research.

The basic items of uniform commence with the army issue 'grey back' shirt that dates back to the Victorian Army. Made of silver grey flannel, the reconstructions follow the original sealed pattern and a surviving shirt, now in the Imperial War Museum. Equally, the original cloth caps are only for museum exhibits and thus all three models must be reproduced from the contemporary patterns. At around £40 each there is the 1902 Pattern Service dress cap known as the 'cheese cutter' due to its wire stiffened rim. For these a member of the *GWS* went to the original factory that agreed to make over forty. The other two caps, the 'core blimey' and the soft topped trench cap, also cost around £40 each. In contrast, original steel helmets are still available for around £60, although care must be taken to distinguish the circular shaped First World War helmet from the more oval Second World War version.

The 1902 Pattern Service Dress jacket is one of the few original items that is available as it continued to be issued and thus manufactured until 1940. These later period items are still available for around £80 and some *GWS* members do utilise them, albeit finding the right size can often be a major problem. Made from khaki serge, it is thus rather ironic that modern reproductions will cost upwards of £150, thus ensuring

On the other side of the lines, these soldiers of the *5 Kompanie, II Bataillon, 916th Grenadier Regiment* march to take defensive positions in the hedges and ditches of the Bocage. Although they took heavy losses in the opening stages of the Battle for Normandy, elements of the 916th fought throughout. Unlike the Jack-booted German soldier of 1940, these grenadiers have adopted the more comfortable ankle boot with gaiters that resembled the British battle-dress.

English Heritage.

those lucky enough to find a 1930s jacket that fits will save a considerable sum. Original brass general service buttons are still plentiful and a full set can be had for as little as £1. The brass shoulder titles can also still be obtained but, depending upon the item, vary considerably in cost. For example, a pair of the standard generic 'Manchester' shoulder titles can be had for as little as £3. However, the specific 'T/8 Manchester' (eighth territorial battalion) can cost over £20 a pair. Original trade badges are also available, a Lewis Gunners or Signallers in cloth or brass can be obtained for as little as £10.

Original First World War trousers are simply impossible to obtain and any that emerge from attics are so fragile they are moved forthwith to museum collections. Rather, members of the *GWS* utilise the readily available 1949 battle dress trousers that are made from the appropriate khaki serge. These simply require a little tailoring, essentially the removal of the patch pocket and the legs taken in. Equally, original boots are unobtainable and modern Royal Navy deck boots at around £20 a pair are utilised as they have leather uppers and lack an anachronistic steel toe cap. Authentic reproductions are available from such suppliers as *Timefarer*, but they can cost in excess of £120 and some members question whether the money is worth the marginal difference in appearance. The

Inside a *Zeltbahn* tent is the typical individual grenadier's kit. The *Zeltbahn* was a triangular shelter quarter that could be worn as a poncho or when buttoned together with another three, made a four man pup tent. The items laid out include the distinctive steel helmet, Y-straps, canteen, gas mask, water-bottle, entrenching tool, bayonet, etc. Tony Dudman.

final item of clothing on the lower torso are the puttees, again made from khaki serge. Surprisingly these were still made until 1995 by the original manufacturer *Fox's* (predominately for footballers). Fortunately the *GWS* heard they were about to cease making them and members purchased their entire remaining stock.

Webbing is a major investment. Although original sets are both available and can still be used, a full set of 1908 Pattern Webb Equipment in good condition and dated to the First World War can cost as much as £500. However, incomplete sets are far cheaper and items such as the bayonet frog and entrenching tool holder are not difficult or expensive to reproduce. As originals are very fragile indeed, anti-gas equipment must be entirely reproduced. Copying originals, a small box respirator and bag costs around £80 whilst one of the simpler gas hoods is around £40. Equally, specialist equipment, such as for Lewis gunners or

Mills bombers waistcoats, must be reproduced. To complete each soldier's equipment, packs contain the numerous personal items required by Field Regulations, ranging from extra clothing to the numerous 'necessaries' such as badges, blacking, laces, brushes, buttonsticks, combs, knives, grease tins, gauntlets, worsted gloves, hose-tops, 'housewives', polishing powder, razor, socks, sponges, pipeclay, spoons, etc.

With the weight of the additional clothes and ammunition that were carried, the packs, along with the rest of the webbing weigh in at around 60lbs. When the members of the *GWS* have undertaken a standard 15-mile route march with all this, it has brought a far deeper understanding of the practical realities of such an 'average' experience and a profound respect for those they portray. It is to be wondered how this compares to those who just read about such exertions from the comfort of an armchair. Members of the *GWS* can personally testify as to how it feels to do the march and then dig the trench before sleeping in it. Waking up with the dawn the following morning provides hard won insight that can take days to recover from.

The basic infantry soldier's weapon is the sturdy wartime version of the magnificent .303 SMLE No.I

Living history is a significant aspect of the reconstruction of the 916th. Here the *Kompanieschneider* (Company Tailor) is hard at work repairing various items of his comrades' uniform clothing. As with all armies in the Second World War, women were taking an ever more active role and in camp, behind the lines, they played a crucial role in helping to keep the soldiers in the field. Tony Dudman.

Mark III*. These can still be held in their original firing condition, albeit on a full part one firearms ticket. They can also be smooth bored for .410 shot gun cartridges and held on a shot gun ticket, or deactivated (a crying shame for any original weapon). All versions cost around £130. With its 18in blade, the 1907 Pattern bayonet and scabbard are readily available for around £25. Where appropriate for their role, a number of members are equipped with the .455 Webley Mark 6 revolver, although due to recent legislation, even though these are original World War One weapons, they must be deactivated to conform to Home Office requirements. Finally, the *GWS* possesses a number of original machine guns that, whilst like the pistols are all deactivated, never fail to impress upon the public these weapons' awesome impact on modern war. These pieces are not cheap, their .303 Vickers gun with its full set of mountings

and tripod cost in excess of £500, whilst each of their two .303 Lewis guns came in at over £800 apiece. Compared to this, their British made .303 Hotchkiss Mark 1 (the French Army's 'Fusil Mitrailleur Mle 09' made under licence at the Royal Small Arms Factory) could almost be called a bargain at around £300.

Moving to the Second World War, the term 'historic re-enactment' usually conjures up, in the eyes of the general public, images of wars long gone, stereotypically cavaliers and roundheads. The unspoken assumption is that the participants are motivated by a desire to re-create aspects of British history. It can therefore raise a few eyebrows to be presented with the spectacle of the re-enactment of events within living memory such as the Second World War, especially when that includes Englishmen uniformed as Germans.

The whole concept of Englishmen choosing to represent a past enemy seems foreign to many. Those that re-enact Bonaparte's blue clad hordes can seem at worst eccentric given the aura of dash and romance that the passage of almost two hundred years now attaches to the Napoleonic Wars in general. Seeking to portray Britain's allies of the Second World War, American or Russian can be viewed as a compliment. However, choosing to portray Britain's mortal enemy

Reminding us that the Battle for Normandy was fought in high summer, these two grenadiers of the 916th have divested themselves of much of their uniform and appear almost relaxed. The soldier on the left still wears his field-grey M1943 service tunic and *Feltmutze*. From his left shoulder hangs the German Army issue torch, whilst he has seen sufficient action to gain the infantry assault badge that is worn on the left breast. His compatriot wears what appears to be a civilian shirt along with the familiar field-grey *Einheitsfeldmutze*. English Heritage.

of 50 years ago with millions still living who lost relations and suffered themselves might, at the very minimum, be seen as in very poor taste.

One society that sincerely seeks to recreate the Second World War, both in terms of living history and combat is *The World War Two Living History Association*. Originally founded in 1978, the present membership is determined to overcome the easy stereotypes and glib criticisms to commemorate the experience and sacrifice of all sides in the conflict. Each year the society stages both public and private events across the country to fulfil these aims. At its public events, living history portrayals are engaged in, with the life of ordinary soldiers in military encampments. These events are often combined with

one or more of the historic vehicle societies. More familiar battle re-creation is increasingly requested, with the intense fighting after D-Day in the fields and hedges of the Normandy Bocage a familiar scenario. The members also stage private-training events that usually involve scripted scenarios, for example the end of the Second World War in a destroyed German town with each individual participant scripted to play a specific role, ranging from a German army deserter, a member of the feldgendarmerie, through to a war weary American GI.

It is at these private events that prospective new members are introduced to the period before participation in public displays. The newcomer has British, American and German units to choose from. For the British there are the Hampshire Regiment, the East Yorkshire Regiment and the 1st Airborne Reconnaissance Squadron. The 505th Parachute Infantry Regiment of the 82nd Airborne Division and the 2nd battalion of the 16th Infantry Regiment that was part of the 1st Division 'The Big Red One' represent the Americans. The Germans field the 5th company of the 2nd battalion of the 916th Grenadier Regiment of the 352nd Division, the 6th Regiment of the 2nd *Fallschirmjager* Division and the 156th *Panzer* Grenadier Regiment of the 116th *Panzer* Grenadier Division. If there are generalised differences as to the alternative characteristics, those portraying Americans tend towards a more relaxed attitude whilst British and Germans tend towards a more professional ethos in the traditional military sense.

David Bennett, a leading member of the society, stresses that in portraying a German soldier he seeks to demonstrate the difference between the Germans and the Nazis. He stresses that no SS formations are represented, especially as it is felt this would inevitably attract very much the wrong sort of individual. Davids own interest was triggered in his youth by Hollywood films where Germans were always portrayed as simplistic thugs whose sole role was to be slaughtered by clean cut Anglo-American heroes. Yet this was a travesty of the truth – they were human beings with their own story to tell. There is also the challenge of accurately recreating and portraying non-English speaking soldiers and doing justice to their memory.

In regard to the attitudes of the general public, far from finding opposition, they express interest in a history for which they feel they have a direct contact through living memory. This is especially true of actual veterans with whom the society has considerable contact and who are generally appreciative. David finds that most allied veterans have considerable respect for the ordinary German

Finally, a far more familiar and desperate image of the WWII German soldier is this recreated Volksgrenadier MG42 gunner somewhere in the Ardennes in January 1945. Despite padded reversible uniforms being more commonly issued by this period, not all frontline units received them. Thus this *volksgrenadier* still wears the field-grey woollen greatcoat.
Tony Dudman.

soldier but this does not usually extend to the SS who were generally regarded as fanatics, a feeling often shared by veterans of the Wehrmacht. The links to the veteran groups is especially strong on the annual field trips to the actual battlefields such as Arnhem, Normandy and the Ardennes. While members of the German units undertake these 'out of kit' for obvious reasons, members of the British and American formations do wear their uniforms. This is particularly true of the 1st Airborne Reconnaissance Squadron that participates each year in the commemorative events at Arnhem.

When it comes to reconstructing the ordinary *Wehrmacht* soldier, it is also the veterans who are often the most important source for information. On the face of it there is an enormous wealth of contemporary material, ranging from official regulations through to period newsreel. However, as with any other historical

period, for soldiers in the field, official regulations were at best advisory and often irrelevant. As for film footage, great care must be taken due to some very dubious editing. All too often, evocative 'action' scenes were and are re-used even if not accurate for the supposed dates of the subject, for example, Tiger tanks destroying T34s in 1941 or the Eighth Army at Normandy! Just such liberties were recently the cause of the 916th having to drop what they had previously thought was their divisional emblem based on supposed footage of the Normandy campaign. On closer examination of the newsreel in question, the location and identity of the vehicle with the previously supposed divisional symbol became very clouded indeed. Whilst Brian L. Davis *German Army Uniforms and Insignia 1933–1945* is something of a bible for guidance, its numerous contemporary photographs reveal the great variety of clothes and equipment actually worn. Consequently, all to often, it is only by talking with the veterans that any conclusive details can be ascertained.

In reconstructing the ordinary front-line German infantry soldier, or *Landser*, of a *Zug* (Platoon) the 916th Grenadier Regiment as he would have been during the late war period of June 1944 to May 1945, David Bennett is rightly proud that over 95per cent of equipment is original. This is made possible by suppliers such as the American based *Lost Battalions*, commercial dealers, military fairs, private collectors and trade between members. For a price, belts, straps, buckles helmets and the like are all available, particularly as good quality reproductions are often only marginally cheaper. Original Y straps costs around £85–90 whilst American made reproductions cost £60. Original belts and buckles average around £50, gas mask canisters (they do not require actual gasmasks) £30–40, ammunition pouches £40, helmets £75–80 and bayonet with scabbard £40. As the 916th is a late war impression, ankle boots rather than jackboots (the latter known as 'Diceshakers' to the troops) are worn. Rather than use expensive originals, modern Royal Navy 'deck boots' are utilised as they have leather soles but no toe cap as per the German version. Although these only cost around £10 per pair, another £20 must be spent to give them an authentic pattern of hobnails. Only the clothes are modern reproductions. Standard M43 field grey tunic and trousers (originally an economy uniform made from re-worked wool, with a heavy rayon content) can be ordered for £240 from America, as can a matching *Feltmutz* (the soft ski cap) for £50. Although the regiment does have two tailors in its ranks, they tend to concentrate on repairs and alterations, though one does make *Feltmutz* for around £25.

With respect to weapons, the vast majority of grenadiers are armed with original Mauser K98 rifles that are held on Part One Firearm Certificates for use with blank ammunition only. Replica MP40s and P38s are also available, but these must be made to approved Home Office requirements for only blank ammunition firing mechanisms. There are only a few MP40s in the 916th given their £450 cost and it can cost several pounds to fire just one clip of 9mm blanks.

The final item for the complete grenadier reconstruction are the various badges that were awarded for wounds, assaults and bravery. So as to ensure that these are not worn indiscriminately, the members of the 916th have agreed specific qualification rules. All grenadiers commence with none. The Wound Badge in black is awarded for a real injury incurred at an event that required medical attention, whilst the Wound Badge in silver is awarded for an injury either requiring an overnight stay in hospital or causing prolonged illness. The Infantry Assault Badge is awarded for ten days of campaigning, that is, five weekend events. The Iron Cross Second Class comes after four years service whilst the Iron Cross First Class is for special accomplishments with the unit. Finally, the War Service Cross, First and

Second Class, is awarded for outstanding non-battle service.

Specialists: Artillery, Cavalry and Surgeons

Alongside rank and file infantry soldiers, there are those one might term specialists, that is, the gunners, cavalry, medics and those who establish and maintain the soldiers' camps.

As Napoleon, undoubtedly the greatest gunner in history, stated, 'It is with artillery that war is made', and with slight alteration, this quote could be applied to any re-enactment from the gunpowder age. Ranging from late medieval wrought-iron breech-loaders, through seventeenth century Sakers, to American Civil War Napoleons, the respective re-enactment societies take pride in their guns. For the public, there is nothing quite like the roar of the guns to get the blood pumping and the hands pressed firmly to the ears. Artillery requires careful handling; for the participants in an action, the area before the cannon mouth is potentially lethal. Even a blank charge wadded with little more than grass will produce a powerful muzzle blast which can burn and smash into anyone foolish enough to stand within 20 or 30 feet of it. Further, cannon and enclosed spaces certainly do not mix: apart from the dramatic amplification of the concussive effect, windows can suffer spectacular and shattering failure, for which both Lincoln Castle and Sandhurst Military Academy can vouch.

Fielding a full size cannon of any period requires a tremendous commitment of time, gallons of sweat and no small financial outlay. It is worth remembering that a full size French Napoleonic 12lb field piece will weigh just under two tons including iron barrel and solid wooden carriage. Sakers of the English Civil War and Napoleons of the American Civil War were of a similar nature. With wheels of over five feet in diameter and a carriage over twice that length, when one adds around seven feet of iron barrel, these are not items that sit in the garden shed or are packed in the boot of the family car. Specially secured garages are often required for storage while vans and trailers are essential for transportation to and from events. Once at events, these pieces need to be dragged into

position, a requirement that leads to some stout individuals being natural born gunners.

Loading and firing a gun requires much practice and teamwork. After each shot, the bore of the gun must be swabbed clear of even the tiniest spark or smouldering debris before a new charge of gunpowder can be loaded. Otherwise, when the rammer is driving the charge to the rear of the bore it may prematurely detonate with catastrophic consequences for the individual. It is for this reason that the primer stands at the breech with their gloved thumb over the vent so as to prevent any draft fanning any potential embers as the rammer acts as a piston. When primed and ready to fire, it is the gun captain's cardinal duty to ensure that there is no idiot standing within the blast area of the muzzle. To signal to other re-enactors that a gun is loaded, one will see a gun captain's right arm raised above their heads: it is the signal to keep well clear.

So how does one go about obtaining a cannon? There are two ways to get guns made. Firstly, they can be faked (as are almost all film and TV cannons), by having a fibreglass or aluminium sleeve encasing a proofed steel liner. This is fairly cheap and allows a very light gun which can safely fire blanks, ideal for film budgets where the weapon will only be discharged a few times and with a small charge just for dramatic effect only. However, given the far harder service demanded by re-enactors whose guns can often be discharged hundreds of times a year, such composite pieces are not suitable. Even after a short duration of use, voids begin to occur around the vent into which powder inevitably seeps. If not addressed, sooner or later this ignites with catastrophic consequences for the sleeve. Such composite guns have been known to blow out beneath the breech leaving a lucky gun crew suffering just shock and concussion. Other incidents, with similar origins, involved the ejection of the steel tube, blown vents and cracked barrels. For serious re-enactors, it is possible to get reproductions accurately made using original designs and traditional materials

By the Tudor period, guns like this Saker had been perfected and had become an essential part of any self-respecting European Army. Alongside the physical damage guns could inflict, was the impact on morale as indicated by the spectacular muzzle flash caught here. English Heritage.

from a number of commercial sources. One of these is the *Irons Bros Foundry* of Woddenbridge in Cornwall that has made dozens of guns in the last 20 years for films, the BBC, English Heritage and re-enactors. For example, they made the full size Tudor Saker, with a three and a half-inch bore, which featured in the *Armada 400* exhibition staged at Tilbury Fort. Such pieces though are very expensive: Roger Emmerson, commander of *Hazards Company* in the *Roundhead Association* recently had a new bronze barrel cast, the cost coming in at over £3,000.

Interestingly, while the supply of cast iron and bronze for casting sixteenth to nineteenth century guns is no problem, a potential difficulty for making an authentic replica of a fifteenth century gun is that they were forged from wrought-iron strip. It is now impossible to obtain this in the sizes necessary in Britain. Fortunately, high-grade wrought iron can be purchased in quantity from Sweden. Reproductions of the sixteenth to nineteenth century guns are still cast

in sand in the traditional manner, the whole process taking up to a week. For the fifteenth century breech-loaded guns, coiling wrought-iron strips into a tube creates the barrels, as it also does the separate chamber pots for the powder charge. Here, the traditional skills of the blacksmith are essential. Meanwhile, the skills of a carpenter and wheelwright are required for making the wooden gun carriages which, depending upon the gun, must be able to carry up to one and a half tons of barrel safely over almost any terrain.

One of the guns featured in this book is a Tudor Saker which was participating in the Armada Tour *Invasion 1588* during 1988. While the Saker was made for the organisers of the tour, *English Heritage*, there was a potential problem in crewing it, given that there was no Elizabethan re-enactment group at that time to take on the part. It fell to an experienced English Civil War gunner, Derek Winder, to take on the role of 'The Master Gunner' and he was able to raise a specialist crew from amongst similar English Civil War gun teams. It is a testament to the professionalism and universality of the re-enactment gunner's art that they were able to undertake an extensive tour, putting on spectacular and entertaining displays of Tudor artillery for the public, essentially from scratch.

The English Civil War witnessed the first large-scale use of cannon on the British Isles. Both on the battlefield and in the numerous sieges, cannon played a crucial role. Here a battery of heavy guns has been placed in a prepared position to bombard the walls of an enemy stronghold. In the foreground is an ammunition box that would be wheeled between the gun and the reserve ammunition wagon some distance to the rear. English Heritage.

The image of the mounted warrior is one of the oldest in military history. Be it the medieval knight, the dashing cavaliers of Prince Rupert, Cromwell's Ironsides, the imposing ranks of Napoleon's Cuirassiers at Waterloo or the dusty blue and grey of American Civil War cavalry, mounted soldiers are fundamental to just about every period of re-enactment. In today's re-enactment societies few are without some mounted component, and not just in Britain, but in France, Germany, Hungary, Russia and America. In fact, for some, such as Hungarian re-enactors, their Hussar units represent the majority of societies, so fundamental is the hussar to their image of history.

For anyone who has either fought in or watched a battle re-enactment, it cannot be denied that even a few mounted men can add significantly to the excitement and spectacle of the event. At the major English Civil War events of both the *Sealed Knot* and *English Civil War Society*, several dozen mounted troopers are fielded, representing Prince Rupert's and Sir William Waller's Lifeguards in the *Sealed Knot*, and Grenville's and Hungerford's Horse in the *English Civil War Society*. Even smaller societies such as the *Napoleonic Association* with its 12th Light Dragoons and Vistula Lancers can field up to a dozen at a time. Probably the largest British cavalry event was in 1992 when the mounted elements of the *Sealed Knot* and the *English Civil War Society* came together to re-stage the first major clash of the English Civil War at Powick Bridge where some 120 troopers and dragoons took the field. In America, the 1988 Gettysburg event saw over 500 mounted troopers in conflict, whilst in Europe, the 1995 Waterloo re-enactment brought together over 200 horsemen from across the Continent.

The attractions of cavalry are obvious, but there are very serious considerations to be taken into account that makes fielding any group of mounted troops a major undertaking. The first is technical, one must be able to ride to a sufficiently high standard so as to be able to safely control a horse in the frightening environment of noise and colour any re-

By the Napoleonic wars, scientific method and decades of experimentation had resulted in lighter, more mobile field pieces capable of throwing 9–12lb shot. Guns that in the sixteenth or seventeenth century would have weighed over two tons now weighed less than one. Here a British Horse Artillery crew have just discharged a 6lb field piece. At full elevation the range of a ball fired from such a gun was now almost a mile due to improvements both in the quality of powder and the strength of the barrel. English Heritage.

enactment involves, while at the same time participating in the 'fighting'. Most societies with their own mounted element maintain a list of members who are trained and tested (British Horse Society Grade two is the basic) and can be allocated a mount. Not only must the rider be trained, so must the horse and there is a limited availability in Britain of such mounts. The second is money; most riders cannot afford to own and transport their own mount so societies have to find the very considerable sums involved, which must include adequate facilities at each event. Even so, the prospective trooper must not only pay for their own uniform and equipment, but must also find the significant amounts of money needed to reproduce the saddlery, tackle and shabraques, which the horse needs if it is to complement the rider's own uniform and

equipment. The third is the question of the safe integration of mounted personnel amongst the vulnerable infantry. It is a testament to the safety of British re-enactment that in over a quarter of a century of existence, there has not been a single recorded serious injury caused by a horseman to an infantryman. However, many riders have had a nasty bruise or two from falling off, much to the amusement of the infantry.

Staging public displays where there is to be a mounted participation brings with it special requirements. Horses need lots of space to function safely in, not only to ensure sufficient room between mounted and dismounted participants, but also to keep well clear of the audience, members of the public having an amazing propensity to poke and otherwise upset the mounts! The larger the display area, the larger must be the viewing area for the audience. The ground itself needs to be firm, without rabbit holes or any other hidden dangers that might do harm to horse and rider, and the land's owner must accept the inevitable damage hooves will cause. Further, horses need to be put out to graze, and with most displays being weekend affairs, horses often appear to have an innate desire to hurt themselves, so it is often desirable to have the services of a vet available. Finally, there

As a testament to the scale and sophistication of today's re-enactors, this Second World War field gun adds an extremely loud element to Second World war re-enactments. Guns such as these played a crucial role in the battle for Normandy in providing indirect fire support. Given their weight though, in utilising such weapons at modern historic reconstructions, it is necessary to have the various vehicles that towed and supported these examples of mid-twentieth century technology. English Heritage.

must be suitable insurance cover, and this, along with all the other requirements, ensures that any event involving cavalry is a major logistical and financial undertaking.

While many societies have their own mounted units, these are inevitably specific to the respective societies' historic period. One of the exceptions to this is *The Troop*, which seeks to achieve a high quality mounted representation in a wide variety of periods. Often working with *English Heritage*, *The Troop* provides a number of mounted representations to add an additional dimension to displays and an example of this is their reproduction of two Roman cavalrymen. The Special Events Unit of *English Heritage* had regularly worked with the *Ermine Street Guard* for many years and it was felt that a mounted

element would be a valuable addition to the display of Roman Infantry. Consequently, English Heritage, as a special project, funded the equipage of two Roman Auxiliary Cavalrymen representing the *Ala I Tungorum* of the third quarter of the first century AD. While the armour and weapons of the troopers came from the *Ermine Street Guard*, English Heritage paid around £500 for each of the contemporary saddles made by the recognised expert in this field, Peter Connolly. Having completed this, the two mounted auxiliaries were able to prove an old Victorian myth very wrong, that without stirrups a Roman cavalryman could not stand the impact of a charge. In fact, the recreated saddles, which have four horns, one at each corner, held the rider so firmly in the seat, stirrups become unnecessary and members of *The Troop* have been able to impress audiences at events with a wide variety of complex manoeuvres. It is also worth noting that great care is taken to provide small horses for these displays, as the mount of the Roman period was noticeably smaller than today's horse.

Living history displays tend to be associated with the domestic side of history. It is all too easy watching battle re-enactment not to see beyond the martial splendour of flashing steel and the blasts of musketry,

126 Specialists: Artillery, Cavalry and Surgeons

By the seventeenth century the age of the mounted knight was truly over, having been replaced by 'regiments' of cavalry in standing armies. The clothes and equipment of the mounted soldier had also been transformed. Although a few items of armour remained, predominantly the helmet and the *cuirass* (there were still a handful of fully armoured *cuirassiers* but they were the exception), the heavy buff coat and jacked boots offered almost as much protection from sword cuts. Indeed, a growing proportion of troopers were dispensing with the *cuirass* altogether as practical experience of charging knee to knee proved that it was the physical impact of an organised and disciplined body of men and horses that counted. Body armour was becoming an encumbrance. English Heritage.

Opposite.

Although cavalry, as a proportion of today's re-enactors, represent a small fraction of the overall numbers, they recreate, alongside the infantry and gunners, the third military arm. Mounted warriors appear in some of the earliest illustrations of warfare and although most think of the legionary when imaging the military might of ancient Rome, their mounted soldiers played a key role in all their campaigns. These two Roman Auxiliary cavalrymen represent the *Ala I Tungorum* as they would have appeared at the end of the first century AD. English Heritage.

By the time of the Napoleonic Wars, body armour was restricted to a few elite heavy cavalry regiments in some European armies such as the French, Austrian and Russian. Rather, the vast majority wore versions of *uniforms worn by the infantry*, as do these troopers of the Twelfth Light Dragoons of 1812–15. Reflecting the influence Napoleon was having even on the British, the general style and cut of these troopers' clothes is unmistakably French, with the bell-topped shako and a short tailed jacket with plastrons that closed to the waist. English Heritage.

but in reality there were horrible deaths and dreadful wounds. For obvious reasons, this aspect of history's conflicts are not displayed on the field and in this respect battle re-enactments are sanitised versions of history. Nonetheless, the bloody side is not totally ignored.

Without doubt, whether ancient Roman, medieval, seventeenth century or Victorian, recreating the detail and reality of past medical practice in the military is one of the most demanding in re-enactment, requiring significant investment in equipment, tremendous attention to detail and an enormous commitment of time. The popularity of medical dramas on television reflects a curiosity with medical matters and in certain respects much the same attraction draws large crowds

to the varied medical re-creations that now enrich living history.

Military medicine dates back to Julius Caesar who had the idea, in 48 BC, of appointing a body of 17 doctors to each legion. These doctors were appointed to the rank of non-commissioned officers so that they were dependent upon the public treasury; thus Caesar created the professional army medical officer. The most numerous, therefore, were the legion doctors, referred to by the name and the number of the legion. Then followed the cohort doctors who treated the praetorian, urban and lookout cohorts. The camp doctors, divided into nurses and surgeons, were assigned the treatment of the garrison soldiers. Rome had also created auxiliary army medical officers who acted as nurses. The most famous of the first army medical officers was Scribonius Largus who accompanied the Emperor Claudius on his military mission to Britain. By the time of the Norman Conquest, the battlefield surgeon was an integral part of any self respecting army, and whilst their ability to deal with the terrible consequences of warfare were restricted to contemporary knowledge, their dedication to relieve suffering is often overlooked.

Chris Jordan, a member of the *Southern Skirmish Association*, portrays a Confederate Surgeon, both on land and at sea. Chris has spent years and invested considerable sums of money to enable him to present an almost exact representation of a Confederate surgeon's medical tent. Today, he has the only fully equipped American Civil War field hospital outside of America. Apart from the canvas of the tent itself, almost everything equipping it is original. The centrepiece of his extensive collection of original items is a large capitol set that includes all the instruments a field surgeon required performing their grisly trade in the field. This was originally made in England and used in the Crimean War. In fact, some 62 per cent of all medical sets used in the American Civil War were manufactured in England. Another series of

This set of 'tools' belonging to a Norman 'surgeon' are almost brutal in comparison to the Roman set. Various probes and hooks were designed to extract arrowheads whilst injuries inflicted by edged weapons were all too often just sutured with twine. The various concoctions in the background were mostly herb-based balms and ointments, although some did have a palliative effect. Philipp Elliot-Wright.

instruments Chris is particularly proud of is an original set once owned by a Dr Johnson, a confederate surgeon of the Trans-Mississippi Army. His other original items include an amputation set made by *Arnold*, a pair of original Civil War Saddle bags still containing original bottles of medicine, including chloroform and ether. There is a duel instrument that operates as both a stomach pump and an enema. There is also a dental set, a medical chest, eye instruments, small medical pocket sets and most fascinating, a scarifyer. This was to draw blood, it being a brass box with a switch. Placed on the arm, when the switch was turned on, 12 blades automatically cut the arm to allow the drawing of blood.

Chris certainly does not try to glorify the activities of a late nineteenth century military surgeon, rather he seeks to educate an audience as to the great leaps forward in medical science and practice made as a result of the American Civil War. The conflict saw the first use of hospital trains to move the wounded and the first organised ambulance corps. The war also progressed the status of women in the medical field: they commenced the conflict as little more than cooks and washer women, but by its end they were assisting in the operating theatre. Having said all this, there was no sterilisation and powerful opiates were required to suppress the agony of even minor operations. One of South Carolina's fundamental contributions to the war was growing these opiates and it was almost inevitable that there was an extensive drug addiction problem after the war. Many crippled soldiers relied on Carolina's opiates to live out their days. With no welfare system the many war cripples, who had originally come from farms, were left selling cloths pegs on street corners for the funds to purchase these drugs.

At public events, Chris and his stewards recreate a number of the contemporary medical procedures including trepanation, amputations and dental work, at times with the liberal use of mostly fake blood and screams. In respect of the latter procedure, Chris also manufactures contemporary false teeth, once originals have been pulled. Equally, a fully equipped Pharmacy

By the seventeenth century, the surgeon's art had made considerable progress as this very full table of surgical instruments, including syringes, testifies. There were now recognised academic and practical qualifications as well as validating bodies in the guise of the Barber-Surgeons Hall. Although they were still ignorant of the needs of hygiene, instruments were at least washed in water and while drastic, rapid amputation of seriously injured limbs did at least mitigate against infection. However, the presence of the dried frog on the right testifies to the survival of a few traditional remedies.
Philipp Elliot-Wright.

Department enables the audience to be educated in what was in each drug, how they helped people and in what ways they were utilised. Mostly this was for the most common cause of death other than wounds: bowel complaints caused by a very poor diet and rampant venereal disease. In fact, so many soldiers fell victim to VD that there were separate hospitals. As for more standard hospitals the war produced one of the largest ever built, Chimber Rosa in Richmond, although nothing remains of its buildings today other than an exhibition of its unique history.

Whilst Chris Jordan portrays an anonymous Confederate field surgeon for public events on land, he also plays a fascinating individual when on *HMS*

Warrior. Each year, members of the *Southern Skirmish Association* utilise the *Warrior* to portray members of the crew of the near legendary Confederate raider, the *Alabama*. When demonstrating to the public the considerable difficulties of being a surgeon on board such a vessel of war, Chris represents the ship's English surgeon, the 26 year old Dr Herbert Llewellyn, the grandson of Lord Herbert. On board ship, given the vicissitudes of naval life, the vessel's doctor was kept busy with a very wide range of illnesses and injuries. These ranged from minor ligament and muscle strains through to serious internal injuries caused by sailors falling from rigging. Equally, sailors were notorious for catching all manor of diseases, from malaria and other fevers during tropical service to scurvy due to the inevitably limited diet prior to shipboard freezers, and needless to say, various types of VD from brief visits to shore-based pleasures. Consequently, Chris recreates a well-stocked infirmary, ready to meet any demand, from balm to soothe a bruised leg, to a full set of capitol instruments to amputate the leg if more seriously damaged.

Chris himself continues to collect original items and is particularly keen to obtain anything belonging to, or associated with, Dr Llewellyn and items of

By the 1860s, significant progress had been made in terms of medical knowledge and treatment. Whilst a little hit and miss, chloroform was at last offering some relief from the pain of the surgeon's knife. However, as this Confederate surgeon's Capital set reveals, amputation was still the most common treatment for serious injuries to the limbs. Equally, stomach wounds almost invariably proved fatal, as little was still understood about infection. Whilst instruments were now being cleaned in vinegar and other disinfectants, this was as a result of hundreds of years of deduction rather than an understanding of microbiology. Chris Jordan.

Confederate naval china. Like so much else, the china was manufactured in England and marked with crossed cannon within a wreath. Unfortunately for Chris, a few years ago he just missed a number of Llewellyn's letters that were auctioned in Atlanta.

To purchase and accurately display the instruments and techniques of the mid-nineteenth century demands considerable funds and a dedication to reading. Fortunately though, original nineteenth century tools are at least still available. However, if recreating a Victorian surgeon is demanding, reproducing the tools of a surgeon of earlier eras requires primary research and skilled craftsmanship, the few surviving original artefacts being museum

pieces which are valued at auction in the region of thousands of pounds. One of the very few to make this commitment is Ralph Needham whose character of a seventeenth century barber surgeon, Master Obadiah Ringwood, is now able to convey to an audience through his unparalleled set of reproduced medical tools an insight into that period's surgery.

Ralph himself is almost a living history artefact having originally joined the *Sealed Knot* just after its creation in 1970. A varied road saw him depart the *Sealed Knot* in 1972 for the *Roundhead Association* and then a complete departure from the hobby during the 1970s and 1980s. When the bug returned in 1991 he rejoined the *Sealed Knot* and found that the intervening years had been unkind and combat a touch straining on the limbs. Consequently it was suggested he might be interested in the somewhat more sedate living history role of a seventeenth century surgeon. Being unemployed at that moment, the time consuming nature of the challenge was welcome and Ralph, with some help from fellow re-enactors, was soon busy in research and reconstruction. Taking the nom de guerre of Master Obadiah Ringwood, Ralph soon found his display was in demand and he was soon adding new characters and periods to his repertoire. Today Ralph makes his living from this, offering

Although such simple scenes as this woman spinning yarn in preparation for weaving from the seventeenth century period may lack the thrill of battle re-enactment, it is a fundamental element of any attempt at broader reconstruction of the past. Such domestic portrayals of living history not only require considerable *research* (often in more depth than many battle re-enactors), but are a reminder of what 95 per cent of the population did throughout history whilst a minority engaged in conflict. English Heritage.

the barbers, who were already a common sight at monasteries cutting monks' hair, so as not to deny this service to their clients. As they worked with their hands they were regarded as tradesmen, and, as was the practice of the medieval world, very soon these barber surgeons formed guilds to regulate their craft. Several centuries later, in 1540, Henry VIII was willing to incorporate the Barber Surgeons Company of London by an Act of Parliament. Their first Master was Thomas Vicary, Chief Surgeon to the King. Under Vicary came the Guilds Wardens who set up headquarters at the Barber-Surgeons Hall in the City of London.

As the surgeon worked with his hands, he was inferior in status to the Physician and doctor who diagnosed with their minds (they had the College of Physicians). However, to qualify as a surgeon was no minor undertaking. To just gain an apprenticeship to a reputable surgeon required a contemporary grammar school education and a 'smattering' of Latin. There followed a minimum of seven years as his Master's indentured apprentice, at the completion of which there was an examination at the Barber-Surgeons Hall. Having qualified, the young surgeon was only granted a limited licence to practice, it being several more years and the reading every six months of a thesis in front of the Company, before he became a Master of Anatomy and Surgery. Only this Master's Degree carried a permanent licence to practice. Even then surgeons were required to attend official lectures and dissections at the Barber-Surgeons Hall to update their knowledge and skills. And that knowledge should not be dismissed. Whilst not knowing why, through observation and rational deduction surgeons knew that if instruments were clean there were 'less accidents', that is to say, deaths. Equally, it was required that all re-used bandages be thoroughly washed.

Taking the above into account, the myth of the ill-educated charlatan who could set up business anywhere is just that, an ill-informed myth. The fact is that to establish a practice in a town required membership of one of the surgeon guilds and if the surgeon did not demonstrate his professional competence, there was soon very few clients. The same was true for the army in the 1650s as General Monk refused to accept a Mr Fish as a surgeon as he had only served a few years as an assistant and had no qualifications. It is this professionalism that Ralph attempts to convey in his portrayal of Obadiah Ringwood. Ralph steers clear of any attempt to carry out fake operations, particularly as even just his talks see the occasional member of the public fainting (five alone during 1997) although he does occasionally

clients at schools, hospitals and numerous public events over a dozen characters and roles to chose from, ranging from a thirteenth century physician to a Second World War Home Guard Sergeant.

Without doubt Obadiah is the most popular character. In portraying the barber surgeon, Ralph's main objective is to educate, and in particular to dispel some of the slurs and myths about surgeons in the past. Far from being the clumsy butchers of stereotype, barber surgeons were as close to qualified professionals as possible in seventeenth century. Dating back to the eleventh and twelfth century, barber surgeons came of age when Pope Alexander the Third decreed at the Council of Tours that it was forbidden for clergy to shed blood. As many clergy were already performing minor surgery, they turned to perform such before an invited medical audience. Instead he explains the daily life and skills required by a seventeenth century surgeon, using his unparalleled collection of reproduced tools and instruments to illustrate the latter. The instruments form the centrepiece of his talks and have taken over six years to assemble. Undertaking research at auctions of original instruments, antique fairs, as well as many visits to museums, with the help of a skilled craftsman, the full range of implements have been hand crafted. Ralph fully accepts that, whilst accurate, there is still room for improvement as he discovers new facts everyday.

In relating the life of a barber surgeon, Ralph attempts to ensure that their contemporary morality is included. They were essentially religious men whose mission was to preserve the living image of the Lord and to serve the sick. Ralph stresses that their moral

code required they serve all, and thus, in the English Civil War, army surgeons attended to both sides. If captured it was accepted by Royalist and Parliamentarian alike that surgeons were freed forthwith. Further, their creed of service to all was respected; after the First Battle of Newbury, although Charles I made it clear he considered captured Parliamentarians as traitors, he equally ensured the Royalist surgeons treated their wounds on an equal footing. For Parliament, Lucy Hutchinson helped Nottingham Castle's parliamentary surgeon dress the wounds of Royalist prisoners, against the opposition of Captain the Reverend Lawrence Palmer, the God fearing, bible-thumping rector of Gedling.

To set against Ralph's serious character of Obadiah Ringwood is his somewhat more tongue-in-cheek portrayal of a thirteenth century medical physician, Sir Ralph of Epperstone (a village near Nottingham). Whilst this portrayal is more of an entertainment, the information and spirit is firmly based in fact. The reason for this alternative approach is simply that to attempt to give a serious tone to a physician of 1210 as he relates his cures is soon lost in the mirth of the modern audience. For example, demonstrating how to cure a headache with Pleintian Root (a common garden weed) tied to the head with a red ribbon (a magic colour), or how to cure cataracts with dried fox's

There is much debate today regarding whether women should be permitted to serve in the frontline. One of Britain's newest living history groups reminds us that for the Soviet Army this question was answered in the Second World War. Here two female members of the *2nd Guards Division* share a drink with comrades surrounded by the paraphernalia of a typical Red Army camp. Remarkably, every single item of clothing, equipment and weaponry in this display are original. Philipp Elliot-Wright.

tongues in a red bag tied around the patient's neck. However, what is conveyed is the importance of the Crusades to the evolution of western medicine, given just how far ahead the Arabs were of medieval Europe. Certainly Sir Ralph of Epperstone acknowledges his debt and thus provides a suitable introduction to his seventeenth century colleague, Obadiah.

As Ralph Needham stresses, whilst recreating the medical world of the past is both fascinating and rewarding, it requires almost as much book study and outlay on instruments as was required of the originals. It is indicative of Ralph's efforts that modern surgeons often form the most attentive of Ralph's audience and as previously mentioned, he is often invited to hospitals to convey the world of the seventeenth century barber surgeon. Here surgeons and theatre staff often comment how the designs of many instruments have not changed through the centuries, many of Ralph's tools being readily identified. Having said this, modern instruments are certainly all custom made for the operating theatre, whilst in the seventeenth century a good friend of any naval surgeon was the ship's carpenter with whom he could exchange saws and chisels.

Before concluding, it would be a travesty not to focus on the crucial aspect of living history, the re-creation of camp life and the populating of historic houses. It is in this context that the historic role of women comes to the fore. In what is in many ways a very male-orientated activity, given its primary focus on the recreation of military history, there is an on-going debate as to whether women ought to be limited to their historically accurate role behind the lines, or whether, given we live in the late twentieth century, women ought to be accepted in the ranks (uniformed and equipped to appear as a 'male' soldier).

Either way, whether it is daily life in a Celtic village, a Norman soldier's camp or a World War One telephonist, the variety of non-military life that is reconstructed is enormous. Requiring as much if not more research when compared to portrayals of soldiers, the depth of everyday life away from the field of battle is fascinating in its detail. Easily overlooked is the need, given the proximity of the public, to recreate not just the clothes, artefacts and habitats of the past, but the richness of social interaction. The apparently simple scene of a Viking woman and her children preparing a meal requires not just the reconstruction from archaeological finds, contemporary illustrations and sagas of cooking implements, but also knowledge of Viking cooking. Equally, when the family sits down, the Viking male must behave to his family, not as in the late twentieth century but as his character would have done 1300 years ago. Given Viking women were the unquestioned rulers of the household, the deference shown to them by the male in this context can surprise the modern audience.

Moving to portrayals of the twentieth century, societies like *Pershing's Doughboys* and the *World War Two Living History Association* now reconstruct in minute detail how the role of women in war has been changing. The *Doughboys* have a fully equipped telephone exchange that would have served as military headquarters within hearing of the trenches of the Western Front, as does The *World War Two Living History Association*. However, reflecting how women are now taking their place on the front-line itself, one of Britain's newest groups, the *2nd Guards Division (Red Army)*, need have no debate about whether it is authentic to have women dressed as soldiers with its portrayal of the men and women who fought side by side in the Red Army in the Second World War.

Re-enactors Directory

Battle Re-enactment and Living History Societies

National Association of Re-enactment Societies

That re-enactment has matured as a hobby was indicated by the formation in 1990 of The National Association of Re-enactment Societies (NARES). In excess of 30 societies belong to this umbrella organisation with a joint membership of over 10,000. NARES acts both as a forum for the exchange of ideas and enables its individual societies to present a corporate face in dealing with the government and safety bodies who are increasingly having an impact on the conduct of re-enactment. Over recent years, NARES has had regular meetings with the Health and Safety Executive as part of the consultative process involved with the preparation of new legal statutes in areas such as the security, transport and acquisition of explosives, safety requirements for the public at events and the preparation of a new code of conduct for historic re-creation. As with many other areas of life today, the impact of European Union legislation is already noticeable in these matters and NARES fully expects to be taking its representation of re-enactment interests to Brussels.

Contact: The Secretary, May Griffiths, Southwood, 318 Cricklade Road, Swindon, Wiltshire, SN2 6AY. Tel: 01793 524465.

Ancient

The Antonine Guard – This small Scottish group recreates the Roman legionaries of the second century AD who built and manned the Antonine Wall.

Contact: John Richardson, 24 Glencoul Avenue, Dalgety Bay, Fife, KY11 5XL. Tel: 01383 825149.

Brigantia – Formed in 1990, *Brigantia* recreates the Iron Age British Celts from the first century BC up to the Claudian Invasion of 43 AD. Dedicated to accuracy and detail its male and female members portray the everyday life of Iron Age Celts, both at home and on the field of combat.

Contact: Karl Gallagher, 67 Palsgrove Road, North End, Portsmouth, Hampshire, PO2 7HP. Tel: 01705 696897 or e.mail: karl@lugodoc.demon.co.uk.

Cohors Quinta Gallorum – A society for research, reconstruction and public display of early third century Roman military and civilian life. They aim to show a different image of the Romans by putting on displays of auxiliary soldiers and all aspects of civilian life with clothes and equipment made using authentic materials.

Contact: Mr VB Griffiths, Chairman. Arbeia Roman Fort, Baring Street, South Shields, NE33 2BB.

The Ermine Street Guard – The oldest, and in many eyes, the best of the Roman reconstruction groups. Formed in 1972, the Guard depicts both legionaries and auxiliary infantry of the Legio XX Valeria Victrix in Britain during the second half of the first century AD, with its major emphasis being on the Flavian period. The Guard's primary focus is the accurate reconstruction of Roman military equipment and the performance of educational public displays. Highly respected amongst academic circles, the Guard's journal *Exercitus* contains both society news and articles on the Roman army written by well-known authors and archaeologists.

Contact: Chris Haines, Oakland Farm, Dog Lane, Gloucester, GL3 4UG. Tel/Fax: 01452 862235.

Gemina Project – Based in Holland, this Dutch group recreates the *Legio X Gemina* in the period of the late first century AD.

Contact: Hesperenzijstraat 20, 5025 KW Tilberg, Holland. Tel: 31-13 536-8325 or e.mail: henk-jan@dds.nl

Legio Secundo Augusta – Reconstructing the Legionary of the late first century AD, *Augusta* stages drill displays and recreates various elements of a Roman soldier's military life. *Augusta* has a number of female members, known under the title *Domina*, who recreate the non-military side of Roman life.

Contact: David Richardson, 61 Totland Road, Cosham, Hampshire, H06 3HS. Tel: 01705 369970.

Vexillatio Legionis Geminae – The men and women of *Geminae* recreate both civilian and military life based around the Roman City of Wroxeter.

Contact: Leonard G. Morgan, 69 The Warren, Hardingstone, Northampton, NN4 6EP. Tel: 01604 763136.

Medieval

Anmod Dracan – A consortium of re-enactment groups aiming to maintain a high standard of authenticity, entertain and educate by living history and combat displays. Crafts demonstrated include all areas of textile production, woodturning, leatherwork, bonework, etc.

Contact: John Watson, Imladris, 224 Coatham Road, Redcar, Cleveland, TS10 1RA. Tel: 01642 489227.

Britannia – *Britannia* was formed with the intention of researching and re-enacting one of the most exciting and turbulent periods in British history that many refer to as the Arthurian age. They specialise in portraying Romano-British military and civil life from the fourth to the sixth century. *Britannia* offers a variety of public displays, from static living history sections showing crafts, food, weaving and armour maintenance, through Latin drill and contact fighting displays.

Contact: Dan & Susanna Shadrake, 13 Ardleigh, Basildon, Essex, SS16 5RA. Tel: 01268 544511.

The Dark Ages Society – A friendly, democratically run group, they aim to accurately portray the period of King Alfred and the Viking invasion – the 870s. Generally arrange non-display events, concentrating on un-scripted fighting. Enjoy a high degree of role-playing that continues at evening banquets that are a feature of DAS events.

Contact: Wayne Osborne, 21 Collington Street, Beeston, Nottingham, NG9 1FJ. Tel: 0115 9257746.

The Escafeld Medieval Society – The object of the Society is to entertain the public and generate an interest in our history by providing the exciting sights and sounds of a medieval tournament, set in thirteenth century England. Raise money for local charities and perform talks for local schools and groups.

Contact: Mrs Irene Deakin, Daledyke House, Bradfield Dale, Bradfield, Sheffield, South Yorkshire, S6 6IE. Tel: 0114 2851233.

Harlech Medieval Society – *Harlech Medieval Society* is a re-enactment group, that, whilst based at Harlech Castle, also performs at other castles throughout England and Wales. Aim is to give an experience of living history and combat within the period 1260–1360 although concentrating on actual events during the wars fought by Edward I.

Contact: Jim Maxwell, Bronheolog, Harlech, Gwynedd, LL46 2YN. Tel: 01766 780648.

The Lincoln Castle Longbowmen – This group aims to recreate late Medieval English life in and around Lincoln and the East Midlands.

Contact: Paul Mason, 54 Grantham Road, Waddington, Lincoln, LN5 9LS. Tel/Fax: 01522 720507.

The Lion Rampant Medieval Re-enactment Society – *Lion Rampant* recreates the era of plate armour from 1300 to 1500. Its members offer the public the opportunity to view the whole span of late medieval life including archery, tournaments, individual combats and dancing.

Contact: Justin Hall, 84b Alpha Street, Slough, Berkshire, SL1 1 QX. Tel: 01753 692159.

The Medieval Siege Society – A living history group that specialises in the recreation of all aspects of medieval sieges.

Contact: Phil Frasers, 70 Markyate Road, Dagenham, Essex, RM8 2LD. Tel: 0181 592 3621.

The Plantagenet Society – Formed in 1975, the *Plantagenet Society* focuses on the fourteenth century. Including men and women, its members demonstrate activities ranging from the use of the Longbow, knights in armour through to medieval dancing.

Contact: Jon Roberts, Jasmine House, Bromsberrow Heath, Ledbury, HR8 1NX. Tel: 01531 650329.

Regia Anglorum – An international society of over five hundred people, dedicated to the authentic re-creation of Vikings, Saxons and Normans (approximately 950–1066). They have an extensive working living history and craft exhibit. Early music, many crafts and their own wooden Viking ship replica, 40ft long with experienced, costumed and equipped crew, are available. Battle re-enactments, involving over 200 people, can be staged, as well as Key Stage 2 school visits.

Contact: Kim Siddorn, 9 Durleigh Close, Headley Park, Bristol, BS13 7NQ. Tel: 01179 646818.

The Vikings (Norse Film and Pageant Society) – Whilst specialising in tenth century Viking-age Britain for over 25 years, their membership have also portrayed Saxons, Celts, Britons, Welsh and Normans from the fifth to twelfth centuries. Provide long term encampments, one-day displays and massed battles, and are experienced in film and television.

Contact: Kevin Orchard, 2 Stanford Road, Shefford, Beds, SG17 5DS. Tel: 01462 812208.

15th–17th Centuries

The English Civil War Society (comprising the King's Army and the Roundhead Association) – The English Civil War Society is a nation-wide organisation dedicated to re-enacting military and civilian aspects of life during the Civil War of the seventeenth century. Events take the form of large battles involving up to 1000 people, smaller skirmishes, drill displays, military and civilian living histories or any combination of these. Events are presented wherever possible on actual Civil War sites.

Contact: For The Roundhead Association – Dr Les Prince, Secretary. 149 Gillott Road, Edgbaston, Birmingham, B16 0ET. For The King's Army – Jonathan Taylor, 70 Hailgate, Howden, North Humberside, DN14 7ST.

The Fairfax Battalia – *The Fairfax Battalia* consists of four individual foot regiments, Devereux's, Fox's, Overton's and Walton's. Basing itself on Sir Thomas Fairfax'

Regiment of Foot, circa 1645, by working together for a number of years, these four units have evolved into a cohesive single unit that has built up a reputation for accuracy and a dedication to 'getting it right'.

Contact: Paul Meekins, 34 Townsend Road, Tiddington, Stratford-upon-Avon, Warwickshire, CV37 7DE. Tel: 01789 295086.

The Free Company – The two dozen men and women of the Company recreate military and social life of the sixteenth century, particularly German soldiers in the service of Edward VI.

Contact: Paul Hull, 19 Down Terrace, Brighton, East Sussex, BN2 2ZJ. Tel: 01273 700025.

The Godolphan Companie – Godolphan's covers the broad period 1400 to 1700, ranging across soldiers, sailors and civilians from the Hundred Years War through to the Restoration.

Contact: Steph Haxton, Star House, Star Corner, Breage, Cornwall, TR13 9BJ. Tel:01326-562908.

The Kynges Ordynaunce – Primarily a specialist fifteenth century artillery group that fields two guns along with soldiers.

Contact: Simon Davey, 545 Wells Road, Knowle, BS14 9AL. e.mail simon@kynges.demon.co.uk.

Livery and Maintenance – An organisation dedicated to re-enacting the Wars of the Roses and Tudor periods. Events range from battle sieges, with authentic camps and artillery, to intensive military, civilian histories, including museum and school presentations. All member groups share a commitment to accuracy and development.

Contact: James Lawson, Secretary. 6 Frew Close, Stafford, Staffordshire, ST16 37B. Tel: 01785 223633.

Ralph Needham – Ralph portrays various periods of medical history, including a medieval physician and a seventeenth century barber surgeon. He has one of the world's largest collections of reconstructed medical tools and instruments.

Tel: 0115 9692922.

The Steel Bonnets Border Rievers – Essentially a specialist Border Reiver living history society, the *Steel Bonnets* portray all aspects of everyday life in the Borders, 1560–1600.

Contact: Neil Tranter, 61 Bexley Drive, Normanby, Middlesbrough, Cleveland, TS6 OST. Tel: 01642 456295.

The Sealed Knot – The *Sealed Knot*, a registered educational charity, is Europe's largest re-enactment society promoting interests in the period of the English Civil War. Activities include: re-enactments of military engagements, living history displays, lectures and school visits, support of research into all aspects of the period and fund raising for the preservation of historic sites and monuments. Where possible, the *Sealed Knot* endeavours to recreate battles on their original sites.

Contact: The Sealed Knot Society Ltd, PO Box 2000, Nottingham, NG2 5LS. Tel: 01384 295939.

The Seventeenth Century Heritage Centre – Although originally formed for living history 1590–1710, we are being increasingly asked to re-enact later periods. Events range from domestic and military living history through to film work, theatrical productions, seminars and talks to schools and interested parties.

Contact: Mrs Jenny Thompson, Chairperson. 25 Connaught Street, Northampton, NN1 3BP. Tel: 01604 27647.

The Siege Group – This small re-enactment group specialises in intimate reconstructions of historical incidents in dramatic form, covering the period of the English Civil War (1642–1651). The Society produces scenarios covering all aspects of life, both military and civilian. The Siege Group bases its historical reconstruction on actual incidents and named characters, whenever possible.

Contact: Dennis Wraight, Flat 11, Marlborough Court, Marlborough Hill, Harrow, Middlesex, HA1 1UF. Tel: 0181 861-0830.

The Stafford Household – This long established group portrays the retained troops of the Dukes of Buckingham during the Wars of the Roses, 1450-1500.

Contact: Graham Smith, 248 Wetmore Road, Burton on Trent, Staffs, DE14 1RB. Tel/Fax: 01283 221122.

The Wardour Garrison – The Wardour Garrison was formed to provide living history events circa 1642 to 1645 at various historical sites. These events cover day to day activities of both a civil and military nature and are produced for, amongst others, English Heritage. The aim is to educate and encourage an interest in the period.

Contact: Dave Allen, 'Leaside', Longmoor Road, Greatham, Liss, Hampshire, GU33 6AG. Tel: 01420 538632.

The Wars of the Roses Federation – This is an amalgamation of groups around Britain that offers a more comprehensive impression of the Wars of the Roses than any single group.

Contact: Paul Clark, 30 Brooks Road, Barrow Hill, Chesterfield, S43 2NN. Tel: 01246 475463.

The White Company – Originally founded to try to dispel some of the myths surrounding the period of history known as The Wars of the Roses, *The White Company* primarily attempts the realistic portrayal of the lives experienced by ordinary men and women in the latter half of the fifteenth century. The society's principal strength is its attention to authenticity and detail that is combined with a friendly 'hands-on' approach to sharing knowledge of the period.

Contact: Mark Griffin, Marketing Officer. 77 Stokefelde, Pitsea, Basildon, Essex, SS14 1NJ. Tel: 01268 462281 or e.mail: dave-key@uk.ibm.com.

The Wolfshead Bowmen – Wolfshead's members specialise in the troops that mustered for the King's Army during the fifteenth century.

Contact: Heath Pye, Rosemary, 15 Tas Combe Way, Willingdon, Eastbourne, BN20 9JA. Tel: 01323 503666.

18th–20th Centuries

The American Civil War Society – Formed in Bolton in 1974 to commemorate the historical connections between Liverpool and the Civil War, the society has evolved into one of Britain's two senior ACW re-enactment societies. All aspects of the conflict are recreated, both military and civilian. The society aims to provide an interesting hobby for its members and to both entertain and educate the public about the war.

Contact: PO Box 52, Brighouse, West Yorkshire, HD6 1JQ.

The Association of Crown Forces (1776) – This American War of Independence society recreates the Coldstream Regiment of Foot Guards of 1775 to the very highest standard. Their primary focus is living history although the group does occasionally participate in battle re-enactments.

Contact: Colin Adams, 13 Greenland Road, Weston-Super-Mere, Somerset, BS22 8JP. Tel: 01934 642441.

The Confederation of Independent American Civil War Re-enactors – The Confederation offers promoters and sponsors tailor made battle re-enactments, static displays and lecturers from the period of the war between the States 1861–1865. We combine a unique blend of living history and theatrical presentation, making each event both educational and entertaining.

Contact: Mrs LG Martin, 241 Kiln Way, Wellingborough, Northamptonshire, NN8 3TN.

The Diehard Company – Formed in 1993 by the Victorian Military Society to provide a living history interpretation of the late Victorian soldier. Reconstructing soldiers of the Middlesex Regiment circa 1881, from its inception this group has gained a reputation as one of Britain's finest living history groups.

Contact: Tim Rose, 21 Addison Way, North Bersted, Bognor Regis, West Sussex, PO22 9HY. Tel: 01234 860036.

The Essex Military Vehicle Conservation Group – The Military Vehicle Conservation Group is a world-wide society with a membership of thousands dedicated to the conservation of all forms of military transport. The Essex branch has around 90 members with over 150 vehicles.

Contact: Colin Tebb, 24 Skylark Walk, Chelmsford, Essex, CM2 8BB. Tel: 01245 251257.

The 18th Missouri Volunteer Infantry – Formed in 1984 as a Federal unit of the Southern Skirmishers, the 18th aims to give as accurate impression of the Federal soldier serving in the western theatre of the American Civil War during the middle part of 1863. The unit strives to reconstruct the daily life of the common soldier either in the field on active campaign, or in a more fixed

encampment setting as befitting the display venue.

Contact: Rod Dawn, 12 Melrose Close, Bordon, Hants. GU35 OXQ. Tel: 01420 474782.

The 21eme Ligne – Formed in 1979, the *21eme* is the largest regiment in the Napoleonic Association. It aims to recreate a standard fusilier company of the late Empire, 1812–15. With over 100 soldiers it is particularly proud of its ability to reproduce, on a one to one scale, the contemporary company drill.

Contact: Chris Durkin, 22 Swallow Street, Oldham, Lancashire, OL8 4LD.

The 33rd Foot (1st Yorkshire West Riding) – Recreating a centre company of the 33rd Foot circa 1812-15, considerable research and preparation has already been carried out to ensure that the uniform, accoutrements and drill of the Regiment are portrayed as accurately as possible. High standards are demanded by this group, as in today's British Army, the 33rd (or Duke of Wellington's) Regiment has the distinction of being the only British regiment named after a person not of royal blood.

Contact: John Spencer, PO Box 187, Halifax, West Yorkshire, HX2 7YZ. Tel: 01422 366451.

The 47th Regiment of Foot – The re-created 47th Foot is a re-enactment society that portrays a Battalion Company of a British Infantry regiment at the time of its service in North America from 1773 to 1777. The society was formed in 1988 by a group of British military history enthusiasts who are all dedicated to the research of the uniform, weapons, equipment and drill of the infantry of King George III's Army.

Contact: Nigel Hardacre, 60 Oakcroft, Woodend, Clayton-le-woods, Chorley, Lancashire, PR6 7UJ Tel: 01772 315192

The 55th Virginia – One of the finest groups representing the Confederate forces of Robert E Lee, the 55th is dedicated to reconstructing the everyday life of the ordinary soldier. Predominately a living history unit, the 55th prides itself on its reconstructed soldiers camps, authentic dress, accoutrements and the excellence of its arms drill.

Contact: Richard O'Sullivan, Flat 11, Grove Lodge, Crescent Grove, Clapham Common, London, SW4 7AE. Tel: 0171 622-4109 or Ken Perry, 61 Boxgrove, Goring by Sea, Worthing, West Sussex, BN12 6BB. The 55th also has a comprehensive website at: www.users.globalnet.co.uk\~jpsykes.

The 68th Durham Light Infantry Display Team – Formed in 1975, the DLI Display Team is recognised as one of the finest groups recreating Wellington's redcoats. Although predominately a living history group that concentrates on reconstructing the everyday life of the soldier and their contemporary drill, the DLI do participate in battle re-enactments.

Contact: Dave Edwards, 9 Academy Gardens, Gainford, Darlington, County Durham, DL2 3EN. Tel:

01325 730795.

The Great War Society – The aim of the Society is to provide an opportunity for practical research into the uniforms, weapons, equipment, training and everyday tasks of the First World War Tommy. Activities focus on living history with members dressing in the uniforms and equipment, learning the drill and undertaking the training and everyday activities of the time. The society is not a battle re-enactment group.

Contact: The Secretary, 6 Station Street, Bingham, Nottinghamshire, NG13 8AQ.

916th Grenadier Regiment – This group reconstructs the ordinary front-line German soldier of the 5 *Kompanie, II Bataillon, Grenadierregiment 916* in the late war period of June 1944 to May 1945. Standards of authenticity are very high and regulations are strictly enforced. they are actively recruiting for 'a few good men' who are prepared to put the time, effort and money into portraying the Second World War German Infantry soldier correctly and without any political leanings.

Contact: 916 G.R., PO Box 156, Loughton, Essex, IG10 1TY.

Histrionix – *Histrionix Eighteenth Century Living History Group* re-enacts social, domestic and military life, both as entertainment and to serve an educational function, including school children. Unpaid, they volunteer their leisure time for the benefit of the society and the historic houses or museums that engage them.

Contact: David Edge, Bromley Cottage, Overthorpe, Banbury, Oxon, OX17 2AD. Tel: 01295 712677.

The Military Music Re-enactors Society – Our society provides musicians to support military living history and re-enactment displays for parade, field music, camp duty and camp concert music used during the Napoleonic and American Civil War periods. The use of period style instruments recreates the correct sound of music.

Contact: Trevor Horne and Dawn Underhill, 17 Booth Street, Handsworth, Birmingham, B21 0NG. Tel: 0121 5548170.

The 2nd Guards Rifle Division, The Red Army of the Great Patriotic War – The 2nd Guards Division (Red Army) is a living history society whose members are dedicated to representing an accurate portrayal of the men and women who served with the Red Army during the Second World War. The society participates in static uniform and living history displays at various military shows. As many authentic items of uniforms and equipment as possible are used, and to be historically accurate, the group actively encourages women to join the ranks.

Contact: Membership Secretary, 21 Elsing Close, Meadow Rise, Newcastle-upon-Tyne, NE5 4SW or Unit Commander, 29 Streete Court, Victoria Drive, Bognor Regis, West Sussex, PO21 2RL.

Colonel George Monck's Regiment of Foot – Monck's Regiment, forebear of the Coldstream Regiment of Foot Guards, seeks recruits to help us bring to life the early history of this famous regiment. We recreate, to a high standard, three different periods, 1650, 1745 and 1815, to enable us to show how the uniform, weapons, equipment and drill of the Coldstream Regiment of Foot Guards changed over time.

Contact: John Litchfield, The Civil Wardrobe, Newtown Road, Newbury, Berkshire, RG14 7ER. Tel: 01635 43806.

The Napoleonic Association – The Association is dedicated to the recreation of a number of regiments that fought in the period 1793-1815, with a reputation for authenticity down to the last button. From April to October each year the Association looks to stage skirmishes of the period in Britain and on the Continent.

Contact: Tony Monks, 77 Dockfield Avenue, Dovercourt, Essex, CO12 4LF.

New France and Old England – Formed in 1996 to recreate the French and Indian War in North America 1755-60, this rapidly expanding society includes British redcoats, French regulars, Woodland Indians and colonials of both sides. The society's activities range from re-enactments of the fierce frontier skirmishes through to detailed military and Indian encampments of both sides.

Contact: Ralph Mitchard, 54 Lower Whitelands, Radstock, Bath, BA3 3JP. Tel: 01761 437543 or e.mail 10644.2623@compuserve.com

Pershing's Doughboys WWI US Army Living History Unit – *Pershing's Doughboys* are a group of enthusiasts dedicated to preserving the memory of the American soldier from 1916–1918. They do this by recreating the image of the American serviceman as he went about his duties. In an effort to give an accurate portrayal of the American soldier, mostly original items of uniform are worn and equipment used. However, some items are impossible to get hold of, only when this is the case are accurate reproductions used.

Contact: Duncan Aran, Pershings Doughboys, PO Box 5265, Weedon, Northampton, NN7 4FB. Tel: 01327 349942.

The Southern Skirmish Association – The *Southern Skirmish Association (Soskan)* is one of the foremost American Civil War re-enactment groups in Britain. Formed in 1968, the aims of the Society are to promote an understanding of the conflict (1861-1865) through living history displays and large-scale battles at major events.

Contact: PO Box 485, Swindon, SN2 6BF.

The World War Two Living History Association – The *World War Two Living History Association* seeks to preserve the uniforms, customs and memorabilia of the ordinary Second World War soldier fighting in North-Western Europe in 1944–45. This takes two forms, public displays of living history and private battle re-enactments. Battlefields, where our original units fought, are also toured.

Contact: David Bennett, 25 Olde Farm Drive, Darby

Green, Camberley, Surrey, GU17 ODU. Tel/Fax: 01252 875412.

Other Related Bodies

The Battlefields Trust – *The Battlefields Trust* is dedicated to the preservation, interpretation and presentation of battlefield sites as educational and heritage resources. As such, it is concerned with battlefields both in Britain and overseas.

Contact: Michael Raynor, Meadow Cottage, 33 High Green, Brooke, Norwich, NR15 1HR. Tel: 01508 558145.

Corridors of Time (Historical Presentations) Ltd – A professional company that has extensive roots in the history of re-enactment. Drawing leading personnel from some ten different societies and eras over the last 30 years, an extensive amount of knowledge and experience is available to those that require a comprehensive cover for the period they seek or enjoy.

Contact: Alan Jeffery, Managing Director, 11 Mulberry Court, Pagham, Bognor Regis, West Sussex, PO21 4TP. Tel: 01243 262291 or Fax: 01243 266721.

English Heritage Special Events Unit – The English Heritage Special Events Unit organises more historical events across England each year than any other body. Between April and October each year in excess of 200 events, ranging from English Civil War re-enactments to craft fairs, classic car rallies and Medieval Tournaments, are staged at 350 English Heritage sites, attracting a total of over 350,000 spectators. The *Special Events* Unit strongly believes in the value and potential of re-enactment in an interpretative role as well as excellent family entertainment. Wherever possible it actively promotes the hobby, especially with official agencies.

Contact: Special Events Unit, 23rd floor, Portland House, Stag Place, Victoria, London, SW1 Tel: 0171 973 3000

The Living History Register – Intended to share research and the authentic methods of any period, they hold a register of skilled re-enactors and produce a bi-annual newsletter to inform all that is available on subscription. The register also provides a comprehensive event diary and details on many merchants and other re-enactment suppliers.

Contact: Roger Emmerson, Publisher, 56 Wareham Road, Lytchett Matravers, Poole, Dorset, BH16 6DS. Tel: 01202 622115.

The Longship Trading Company – *The Longship Trading Company* is a professional company that specialises in dramatically bringing alive Anglo-Saxon and Viking England through the following. Interactive education workshops on schools and museums (Keystage 2). Authentic living history craft demonstrations and the manufacture, production and sale of an extensive range of everyday early medieval artefacts and supporting materials.

Contact: Simon Blackmore, Secretary, c/o 342 Albion Street, Wall Heath, Kingswinford, West Midlands, DY6 OJR. Tel: 01384 292237.

Suppliers

The best way to gain access to the vast array of suppliers of reconstructed clothes and equipment is to join one of the societies and take advantage of the their 'merchants row'. The following list reflects some of the key suppliers to the societies mentioned in this book, although this must not be taken as a specific recommendation. Equally, this is as complete a list as it has been possible to compile given the somewhat disparate and eclectic nature of the craftspeople concerned.

Ages of Elegance – Makers of historical clothing. 6 Cromwell Road, Teddington, Middlesex, TW11 9EH. Tel: 0181 977 9160.

Ancestral Instruments – Various historical bagpipes, redpipes, hornpipes, bag hornpipes, medieval fiddles, rebecs, lyres. David Marshall, Tudor Lodge, Pymoor Lane, Pymoor, Ely, Cambs. CB6 2EE. Tel: 01353 698084.

Armour Class – Supplier of reproduction/re-enactment weapons and armour. 193a Dumbarton Road, Clydebank, Glasgow, G81 4XJ. Tel: 0141 951 2262.

Bailiff Forge – Manufacturer of seventeenth century swords, armour and accessories. Unit 53, Colne Valley Workshops, Linthwaite, Huddersfield, HD7 5QG. Tel: 01484 846973.

Alan Beadle – Specialist dealer in original Antique Arms and Militaria. Catalogue available from PO Box 168, Dorchester, Dorset, DT2 9YD. Tel: 01308 897904.

B & L Collectibles – Stockists of twentieth century militaria. 95 Holyoke Street, Easthampton, Massachusetts, MA 012027, USA. Tel: 001413 5275788.

Black Hawk Armour – Supplier of a complete range of Roman Lorica Corbridge 'Type A' components, plates and fittings. 28 The Dale, Thundersley, Essex, SS7 1TD. Tel: 01268 753318.

Bodgerarmour – Superb quality manufacturer of sixteenth and seventeenth century weapons, cutlery and living history items in general. The East Barn, Moulton St Mary, Norwich, Norfolk, NG13 3NQ. Tel: 01493 751756.

Caliver Books – This book shop carries one of the UK's most comprehensive listing of all periods of military history. 816-818 London Road, Leigh-on-Sea, Essex, SS9 3NH. Tel: 01702 73986.

Campaign Arms – Firearms dealer, gunsmith and explosives engineering. We also stock a wide range of specialist supplies. PO Box 12, Stanford-Le-Hope, Essex, SS17 7AE. Tel: 01375 640664.

The Civil Wardrobe – Supplier of seventeenth to nineteenth century clothing, leatherwork and accessories. Newtown Road, Newbury, Berkshire, RG14 7ER. Tel: 01635 43806.

County Cloth – Maker of some of the best American Civil War uniforms, being renowned for their correct cut and colour. Charlie Childs, 13797C, Georgetown Street NE, Paris, Ohio 44669, USA.

The Drop Spindle – Supplier of seventeenth century costume and spinning supplies. 35 Cross Street, Upton, Pontefract, WF9 1EU. Tel: 01977 647647.

Eagle Classic Archery – We stock a range of well made inexpensive longbows. A colour catalogue featuring our full range of traditional bows, arrows, quivers, replica medieval arrows, arrow heads and Barnett crossbows is available. 41 Spring Walk, Worksop, Notts. S80 1XQ. Tel: 01909 478935.

The English Armourie – Supplier of steel armour, matchlocks, doglocks and all seventeenth century shooting accessories. Dept.10, 1 Walsall Street, Willenhall, West Midlands, WV13 2EX. Tel: 01902 870579.

English Civil War Shoes – Supplier of both seventeenth century open-sided latchet shoes and closed-in sided soldiers' shoes. Pinnocks Farm, Northmoor, Witney, Oxon, OX8 1AY. Tel: 01865 300626.

Kevin Garlick – Maker of historic period shoes of all periods. 21 South Street, Ventnor, Isle of Wight, PO38 1NG. Tel: 01983 854753.

Great War Militaria – Stockist of almost all-conceivable items associated with WWI. PO Box 552, Chambersburg, Pennsylvania, USA. Tel: 001717 2646834.

C & D Jarnagin Co Ltd – America's oldest established American Civil War re-enactment clothing supplier, including leather accoutrements, footwear and tinware. PO Box 1860, Corinth, MS 38834, USA. Tel: 6012 871977.

Sarah Juniper, Cordwainer – Maker of high quality handsewn boots and shoes of all historical periods. 109 Woodmancote, Dursley, Gloucestershire, GL11 4AH. Tel: 01453 545675.

Victor James – Manufacturer of re-enactment equipment, including baldricks, scabbards, belts and tents, works in metal, wood, canvas and leather. 15 Whitmore Road, Chaddesden, Derby, DE21 6HR. Tel: 01332 663432.

Herts Fabrics – Supplier of cloth to re-enactors, from Vikings to the American Civil War. 11 Brickfield, Hatfield, Herts, AL10 8TN. Tel: 01707 265815.

Roy King – A professional Armourer with over with over 25 years experience specialising in European Arms & Armour. For a catalogue containing over 150 illustrations of swords and more than 50 pieces of armour and helmets contact Roy King, Sussex Farm Museum, Horam, Nr.Heathfield, East Sussex, TN21 OJB. Tel: 01435 813733.

Andrew Kirkham – Supplier of quality longbows in Ash and Lemonwood, authentic crossbows with steel prods, along with a full range of hand-forged arrowheads, fire equipment, candlesticks and ironwork, daggers and eating knives. 60 Leedham Road, Rotherham, South Yorkshire, S65 3EB. Tel: 01709 540390.

Military Metalwork – Maker of fine quality historical uniform, costume, accoutrements and regalia. 1 Almond Grove, Brentford, Middlesex, TW8 8NP. Tel: 0181 568 3210

Marcus Music – Maker and repairer of early musical instruments, including military drums. Tredegar House, Newport, Gwent. Tel: 01633 815612.

Paul Meekins – Specialist stockist of second-hand military books. 34 Townsend Road, Tiddington, Stratford-upon-Avon, Warwickshire, CV37 7DE. Tel: 01789 295086.

Norman D. Landing Militia Sales – Specialist in most twentieth century militaria. Mr Ken Lewis, Warley Woods, Warley, West Midlands, B67 5EH.

Past Tents – Manufacturer of high quality reproduction tents for all historical periods. High View Bungalow, Main Street, Clarborough, Retford, Nottinghamshire, DN22 9NJ. Tel: 01777 869821.

The Plumery – The only manufacturer of horse hair, feather and wool military plumes in the world. They also manufacturer quality reproduction Napoleonic Shakos. The Plumery, 16 Deans Close, Whitehall Gardens, Chiswick, London, W4 3LX. Tel: 0181 995-7099.

Seals (Adam the die cutter) – Fine quality medieval seal matrices, all hand engraved to your requirements. Send SAE to: 174 Bedminster Down Road, Bedminster Down, Bristol, BS13 7AF. Tel: 0117 9668856.

Timefarer Footwear – Supplier of high quality historical footwear. Bainbridge, The Square, Timsbury, Bath, BA3 1HY. Tel/Fax: 01761 471430.

Ken Trotman Ltd – Supplier of books on military history and antique weapons. Unit 11, 135 Ditton Walk, Cambridge, CB5 8PY. Tel: 01223 211030.

The Two "J's" – Manufacturer of seventeenth century swords, baldricks, polearms and military leatherwork. 32 Ashfield Drive, Anstey, Leicester, LE7 7TE. Tel: 01533 363514.

Yorkshire Historic Arms – Manufacturer of seventeenth century muskets, musketeers' equipment and pewterware. 14 Anvil Street, Brighouse, West Yorkshire, HD6 1TP. Tel: 01484 716130.

19th Century Tailoring – Britain's largest supplier of American Civil War re-enactment equipment including haversacks, cap pouches, cartridge boxes, buttons and buckles. Manufacturer of high quality clothes from the Napoleonic through to the Great War period. 13 Kinsbourne Avenue, Bournemouth, Dorset, BH10 4HE. Tel: 01202 537110. e-mail: rbz@globalnet.co.uk

Bibliography

As much of the technical/historic information was supplied by the respective societies that are highlighted in this work, the following bibliography is necessarily limited.

Bull, Stephen, *World War One: British Army*, Brassey's, 1998.

Chartrand, René, *Napoleon's Army*, Brassey's, 1996.

Davis, L. Brian, *German Army Uniforms and Insignia 1933-1945*, The Military Book Society 1973.

Drury, Ian, *Confederate Infantryman 1861-1865*, Osprey, 1993.

Edge, David and Paddock, John Miles, *Arms and Armour of the Medieval Knight*, Guild Publishing, 1988.

Elliot-Wright, Philipp J.C., *English Civil War*, Brassey's, 1997.

Field, Ron, *American Civil War Confederate Army*, Brassey's, 1996.

Fletcher, Ian, *Wellington's Army*, Brassey's, 1996.

Fosten, DSV, *The British Army 1914-18*, Osprey Publishing Ltd., 1978.

Gravett, Christopher, *The Norman Knight 950-1204 AD*, Osprey Publishing Ltd, 1993.

Hackett, General Sir John, *Warfare in the Ancient World*, Sidgwick & Jackson Ltd, 1989.

Hadden, R. Lee *Reliving the Civil War – A Reenactor's Handbook*, Stackpole Books, 1996.

Haythornthwaite, Philip J. *British Infantry of the Napoleonic Wars*, Arms and Armour Press, 1987.

Kimmel, Ross M. *The Confederate Infantryman at Antietam, 1862*, Military Illustrated, Vol. 17, February/March 1989.

Koch, HW, *Medieval Warfare*, Bison Books Ltd., 1982

Koch, HW, *The Rise of Modern Warfare 1618-1815*, Bison Books Ltd, 1981.

Nicholls, Ph.D. David, *Arthur and the Anglo-Saxon Wars*, Osprey Publishing Ltd, 1984.

Peachey, Stuart and Turton, Alan, *Common Soldier's Clothing of the Civil Wars 1639-1646 Vol.1*, Stuart Press.

Ritchie, W.F. and JNG, *Celtic Warriors*, Shire Publications Ltd, 1985.

Robinson, H. Russell, *The Armour of Imperial Rome*, London, 1975.

Shadrake, Dan & Susanna, *Barbarian Warriors–Saxons, Vikings and Normans*, Brassey's, 1997.

Smith, Robin, *American Civil War Union Army*, Brassey's, 1996.

Sumner, Graham, *Roman Army-Wars of the Empire*, Brassey's, 1997.

Willing, Paul, *Napoléon et ses Soldats – 1804-1809*, ler Tome, Musée de l'Armée, 1986.

Willing, Paul, *Napoléon et ses Soldats – 1810-1815*, 2e Tome, Musée de l'Armée, 1987.

Windrow, Martin and Embleton, Gerry *Military Dress of North America 1665-1970*, The Military Book Society, 1973.

Index

Acknowledgements

This work would not have been possible without the willingly co-operation of numerous re-enactors, be they those who patiently answered all my numerous inquiries and permitted me to utilise their own written material, willing checked the text to correct my historical inaccuracies and particularly those who supplied the excellent photographs that illustrate this work. Particular mention must go to Chris Haines of *The Ermine Street Guard*, Karl Gallagher of *Brigantia*, Dan Shadrake of *Britannia*, John Cole and Ian Jeremiah of *Conquest*, Dave Key and Mark Griffin of *The White Company*, Paul Meekins of *The Fairfax Battalia*, Keith Raynor of the *33rd Foot*, Chris Durkin of the *21eme Ligne*, Colin Wright of the *18th Missouri*, Richard O'Sullivan of *Company F, 55th Virginia*, Duncan and Howard Aran of *Pershings Doughboys*, Geoff Carefoot of *The Great War Society* and David Bennett of *The World War Two Living History Association*. Appreciation must also be expressed for the pioneering work of Stuart Peachey and Alan Turton in respect of the reconstruction of English Civil War clothes and equipment. May I also extend my thanks to the *Special Events Unit of English Heritage*, especially Howard Giles, Thomas Cardwell and Alisa Williams. Finally, my deepest gratitude to my wife Caz for both putting up with my many hours on the computer and for being willing to check through the finished text to correct my numerous spelling and grammatical errors.